FITRA JOURNAL:
THE MUSLIM HOMESCHOOL QUARTERLY

First Edition, 2016

Copyright 2016 Fitra Journal
www.fitrajournal.com
Editor: Brooke Benoit

Design by Reyhana Ismail
www.reyoflightdesign.com

All rights reserved. No part of this publication may be reproduced in any language, stored in any retrieval system or transmitted in any form or by any means - electronic, mechanical, photocopying, recording or otherwise - without the express permission of the copyright owner.

CONTENTS

Getting Started: Brooke Benoit..4

CHAPTER 1: WHERE TO START..7
Do You Have A Homeschooling Mission Statement?: Priscilla Martínez........................8
Getting my Husband to Agree to Homeschooling: Karima Heraoua..........................10
A Guide to Getting Started: Umm Ibrahim Samirah..13
How To Create A Homeschooling Budget: Ismail Kamdar..21
Learning to speak their Language: Klaudia Khan..24
A Teen's Mid-Education Mindshift: Iqra Arfeen..28
From Bullied to Blossoming: Isra Arfeen..30

CHAPTER 2: THE FUNDAMENTALS..33
Designing Your Family Culture: Chantal Blake..34
Understanding Child's Play: Saira Siddiqui..37
We *Can* Homeschool Arabic And Islamic Studies: Zakiya Mahomed-Kalla...............40
Quality Time - Putting 'Home' Back Into Homeschool: Asma Ali...............................44
A Peek at a Day: Azra Momin..48

CHAPTER 3: SOCIALIZING, SUPPORT AND SELF-CARE..................................53
Yes, Socialization Can Be a Problem: Jamila Alqarnain..54
Finding the Right Pillars of Support: Angeliqua Rahhali...56
12 Steps to Practicing Vital Self-Care: Khalida Haque...60

CHAPTER 4: FURTHER OUTSIDE THE BOX..67
Single-Parent Homeschooling: Samar Asamoah..68
At Last, Homeschooling My Child With Dyslexia: Ann Stock Ghazy..........................70
Why I Still Homeschool in a Muslim Country: Brooke Benoit....................................74
Unschooling in Pakistan: Sadaf Farooqi..77

CHAPTER 5: RESOURCES WE LOVE...81
Review - Homeschool 101: What to Expect Your First Year: Brooke Benoit...............82
Review - Miraj Audio: Chantal Blake..84
Fitra Contributors' Ultimate Resources: Multiple...86

Editorial: Getting Started

Brooke Benoit

For a few years now, people have suggested that I write a book about homeschooling. *Why would I do that?* I thought, *What do I know about homeschooling?* Well actually, quite a lot. Over thirty years ago, I first became fascinated by the concept of homeschooling (and democratic schools) as a child when a handful of then rare homeschoolers and the Sudbury school were making the rounds on daytime and news-magazine TV shows. I was an inquisitive, creative and intelligent child who was beginning to experience school burnout at around age ten. My school had enrolled me into the gifted program, but even that was a disappointment as it felt like more of the same. I was eager to explore my own varied interests and at my own rapid pace; in a few more years I would leave high school to do it.

"I'm not dropping out," I assured my mom the day I came home and (somewhat dramatically) insisted that I wouldn't return to my high school, ever again. I wanted to continue my education, "... but not there and not like that." I wanted to go to college and didn't see the point in sitting through three years of boring and often redundant highschool material first. Turns out there was another way and at fifteen years old I began taking college courses concurrently while enrolled in a take-home program for "at risk" high school students. I passed my GED equivalency the following spring and began college full-time.

It would be many years, even after I began to homeschool my children, before I realized that I had homeschooled – technically unschooled – myself. I was actually quite shocked to be in the position of considering homeschooling for my children. I simply hadn't thought of educating them in anyway different than the sweeping norm of brick and mortar school. But once faced with the pending enrollment process, I knew I had to do something else. Funnily enough, in his book *Homeschooling 101: What to Expect in Your First Year,* Ismail Kamdar describes a similar experience of using an alternative schooling method for himself, but not recognizing it as it is: a viable alternative for many families, including his own kids. This is how deeply ingrained contemporary schooling is in our human joint psyche. Even though we *know* it's a relatively new and even proven-flawed form of education with often disappointing and damaging results, we have all been effectively institutionalized to *feel* that school is the only way to educate children, and to be fearful of doing anything different.

I often hear from non-homeschoolers, "I could never do it!" and I wonder what "it" is. What do they think I do all day? I don't think I do what they think I do. My family's homeschooling style certainly isn't a 9-3 kind of thing. It's a 24/7 kind of thing- but isn't all parenting? Still, now that I have been familiar with homeschooling methods and families for two decades and then some, I know that there are many ways to educate your children outside of school walls. As Angeliqua Rahhali says in her article in this issue on building support networks, "You create the learning environment you want that works best for your family." And that is basically why I didn't feel I could write a book about homeschooling. Not only is my style non-definitive of the immense ways and means you can homeschool, it is also constantly evolving as my family evolves. As Priscilla Martínez says in her piece on crafting a mission statement, "Flexibility in a family, but especially in a homeschooling family, is key." I simply don't feel that my experience is enough to extrapolate homeschooling to all the families who are so desperate to learn how to do it and do it the right way ... *and yet, my children are second generation homeschoolers ... and as a writer I especially have quite a lot to say about homeschooling... and I certainly know an awful lot of Muslim homeschoolers who also know a lot about homeschooling ... and I have a few years experience curating other people's stories as a magazine editor...* and finally I had my ah-ha moment! A Muslim homeschooling magazine was exactly what I should do.

Welcome to the first issue of *Fitra Journal – The Muslim Homeschool Quarterly*. Whether you are just looking to keep your children out of preschool, pulling them out temporarily or committed to the long haul of home-educating, Insha Allah, within these pages you will find the inspiration and camaraderie you need on your own homeschooling journey. In this and future issues, our contributors hail from around the globe and are sharing the wisdom and experiences to help all of us find and enjoy the successes that come with Muslim-centered homeschooling.

Thank you so much to everyone who has shared their story with *Fitra Journal* and the folks who kept pushing me to share mine, especially Aaminah Shakur, Aisha Koolen (she even suggested a magazine!) and always my encouraging and supportive mom, Sandie Benoit. A huge thank you to Reyhana Ismail who kindly volunteered to help me produce this much-needed resource.

May Allah (subhanahu wa ta'ala) allow *Fitra Journal* to help you to recognize and nurture your child's pure state and true purpose, ameen.

Brooke Benoit, Founding Editor of Fitra Journal | editor@fitrajournal.com

Chapter 1
WHERE TO START?

Do You Have A Homeschooling Mission Statement?

By Priscilla Martínez

Whether you're striving to live a life that's more mindful, more purposeful, or more intentional, writing out your goals and vision will undoubtedly help you to get there. Some folks call this a mission statement, which Google defines as "a formal summary of the aims and values of a company, organization, or individual."

Way back when hubby and I first decided to homeschool (before we even had our children), one of the best pieces of advice we were given was to create a homeschooling mission statement. We did and it's changed a lot over the years. I mean a lot. And that's okay. *We've* changed a lot. And our six kiddos have also changed a lot. Our family's goals have evolved. Our children's needs have transformed. So we, as parents, have adjusted our goals. And our family has adapted. Flexibility in a family, but especially in a homeschooling family, is key.

It may seem contradictory that I stress being flexible and having a mission statement (which seems inherently firm) at the same time. The truth is that as a homeschooler, you'll need both. I highly encourage you to start thinking about what you would put in your own homeschooling mission statement - regardless of where in life you are right now. You'll need to turn to it during the good times ("Yay, we're on course!") and during the not-so-good times ("Remind me again why we're homeschooling?!").

And if you're not homeschooling, then write one for your kiddos' education. If you don't have children yet, write up a personal mission statement for five years from now, ten years from now, and so on.

The best part is that there is no wrong mission statement. It can be as detailed or as broad as you wish. You can focus on goals to be met within a specific timeframe, or you can focus on broad, intangible aspirations. You can borrow ideas from others, but you should make sure that your statement ultimately reflects your (and your family's!) unique goals.

Here's our homeschooling mission statement to get you thinking about what you definitely do or definitely do not want to include in yours. Feel free to use this as a starting point to get you brainstorming. Then just run with it!

Our approach to homeschooling is holistic. We do not separate the myriad of activities that ebb and flow throughout our days (and weeks, months, & years) into "this is school" and "that is not school." Our goals as parents are general, so our work toward those goals focuses on the big picture. We want our children to be capable of tackling challenges and to understand and appreciate the value of hard work. We want them to be upstanding members of society who are involved with and contribute to the communities around them - our family, our neighborhood, our mosque, our country, our world. We believe that the most important attributes we can foster within our children are a love of God, a love of learning, a willing heart & mind, and confidence in knowing that if there is something you don't know, you can always learn!

We have not found a packaged curriculum that meets our family's goals and we don't believe one exists. We seek out individual resources that enable us to piece together the subjects that our children are most interested in (sprinkled with gentle nudges toward those that we believe are most critical!), allowing them to pursue their interests at their own paces, which has resulted in what would be labeled as unschooling. Because we also strongly believe in learning through experience, we have made it a priority to travel as a family. (So far, we have been fortunate to be able to travel with our children to Germany, Hawaii, France, Mexico, Italy, Bermuda, The Bahamas, and Canada, among other places.)

Each of our children learns and grows at their own pace. We cherish that individuality and encourage others to embrace it in their relationships with their own children. We are pleased and grateful that, due to our proactive approach and the opportunities we've been blessed with, our children truly know people who are "different" from them simply as fellow members of the human family. Everything we do - whether visiting various places of worship (we have a favorite synagogue we call "our synagogue"), hosting religious leaders or government officials, participating in print or video interviews with the media, learning alongside fellow homeschoolers in classes and co-ops, working toward ranks in Scouting, or just monkeying around in sports - supports our firm belief that "What is most important and valuable about the home as a base for children's growth into the world is not that it is a better school than the schools, but that it isn't a school at all. [John Holt]"

Priscilla Martinez is an unschooling mama of six for more than 18 years, aromatherapist, herbalist, chickenkeeper, author-activist for more than 20 years, and the voice behind Salam Mama.

This article is reprinted with Priscilla Martinez's permission. It originally appeared on her website Salammama.com.

Getting My Husband To Agree To Homeschooling

By Karima Heraoua

This is my story about how I managed to get my husband to agree to homeschooling our children - something I had wanted to do for many years. He was firmly against me homeschooling due to how he saw schooling. We come from different backgrounds. Schools in his native region of North Africa were very strict and he had to pass yearly tests before he moved up to the next class. It was very regimental. In the school system I was brought up with in the United Kingdom we were always in the same class as those of the same age no matter the ability.

Through personal involvement with my own children's school experiences, I noticed how the system was struggling to cope with different children's needs. My son (first born) was a September baby and very advanced for his age. He struggled in school and became disruptive because the work was too easy for him. A school psychologist was brought in to see him at the age of four, at the end of his first year of two years of nursery education. They told us that the issue lay with the nursery and not my son. The nursery was not meeting his needs and they warned that we would struggle with this issue throughout his education if the schools were not prepared to properly engage with him.

As new parents this was quite a shock to both me and my husband. We looked for a school with smaller class sizes, as UK school class sizes are about 30 children to one teacher. We found a school with only 15 pupils in the class and we thought that this would work. He still continuously struggled depending on which teacher he had. Some teachers loved his keen interest and flawless assignments, yet some disliked that he struggled to stay patient when he found things boring. These combative teachers expected all children to do the same work and be satisfied with it. We tried the school for five years, then he moved into the secondary school where it was back to 30 pupils in a class. Every year had its challenges and I found myself regularly visiting the school for different issues. My son deeply hated school but his father insisted that it was the only way to be educated.

I approached the topic of homeschooling many times but my husband always said no - I guess he was fearing moving away from the norm, as he had never heard of anyone doing this before. In addition to my son we have two daughters who didn't really have any major issues at school - they fitted in quite nicely. When I had my first daughter, while my son was in nursery, I went to college to study and get a certificate as a teacher's assistant. I had to work in a school environment as part of the course. This opened my eyes as to how the school system works. I realised how many flaws there were in the system and that even if you have the best, most motivated teacher they do not have the time to assess and monitor every child in the classroom due to workload and distractions. This is when I first realised why my son wasn't coping well and believed there must be another option. I went home, did some online research, and found out about homeschooling.

I approached my husband with the possibility of homeschooling, but he was adamant that it wasn't going to happen. I did this yearly. The moment that it really hit me that I couldn't let my children be in school anymore was when it was time for my eldest daughter, then 11 years old, to start secondary school. My son, who was then 14, filled me with horror stories about what happens in school. Not just the teaching problems, but children involved with sex, drugs, bullying, etc. My son knew that at his age his dad wasn't going to change his mind about homeschooling him as he was already prepared for his exams, but my son really thought it was a good idea to keep pushing for me to homeschool the girls. I had weeks of worrying about what would happen to my daughter, especially as where we live there are no other Muslims and she would be the odd one out. This hadn't really bothered her in her primary years but the transfer to secondary would mean mixing with more, and different, people.

I knew it wasn't going to be easy approaching my husband after all these years of him refusing, so I joined many online homeschooling networks and looked for advice as to what I could do to change his mind. I eventually came across a new approach. I printed off many reports, more than a hundred pages - too many to read. These were about all the good points of homeschooling, then to be fair I printed off a list of cons too just to keep him happy. Also following advice, I decided to ask for a trial period so at least then he felt as if he had some control in the decision: I think this is important to some men and was crucial for me.

I told him that I needed to have a serious talk with him. We set some time aside when the children were in bed so as not to be disrupted. I gave him the huge pile of reports and said to him that I was really serious about homeschooling both our girls, but especially the eldest and that I did not want her to start the secondary school. I have to be truthful and say he wasn't impressed. I then explained that I knew he had doubts and that to be honest I might start this path and not be able to make it either, but I had to at least give it a try. I told him that even if we both agreed to a trial period, if it didn't work out, it really wasn't going to be a big difference in the girls' schooling as they are both fairly bright anyway. He still wasn't too impressed, but he did seem to like the trial part of the deal. I then gave him an ultimatum, too. Yes, I know I was a bit naughty, but I had to let him know I was very serious on this matter! I told him if he didn't agree, I would refuse to take the girls to school in the morning and refuse to collect them from school too. This is something I have always done and many parents will know it isn't a easy job, especially in the rain and snow. I told him to think it over but not make me wait too long.

After about three days he came back to me and said that he only looked at a couple of the pages, as I guessed, but that he would agree to a trial of two or three school terms to see how it goes. You can't believe how happy I was after all these years of asking! All I had to do was put the ball in his court and make it look like he was in control. I so wish I had thought of that approach years earlier. He did say that I had to follow the curriculum as part of his acceptance, which I agreed on.

When the time came in July for school to end I handed in the de-registration forms, which is a requirement in the UK. I was so relieved and my daughters were so happy. They did enjoy school, but they also wanted to try homeschooling and they suspected the benefits of it.

When September started my husband expected them to start their school work at 9:00 am just like in school and finish at 3:00 pm. He was at work all day and didn't know what was happening. At first, to keep him happy, I did make sure the girls kept busy with their studies most of the daytime. My husband was still very apprehensive about our decision and he refused to inform any of his family abroad that we had taken the girls out of school. He also didn't tell his friends about it as he probably thought it wouldn't work out. So as best as we could, we kept it a secret. And he didn't like the girls coming into his workplace (he is self employed) during the day in case any customers started asking questions. Once the end of the year approached I was getting a little stressed myself, wondering what he was going to say. I was still ready to tell him that if he wanted them in school he had to do everything, including prepare packed lunches, and buy uniforms!

However, I shouldn't have worried as after the year was up and he saw that we were coping fine and he was happy with the amount of work they were doing, he was relaxed. He saw how happy the girls were and how it was also nice not to worry about them missing any work. At school if the girls were off sick, they never got caught up and simply missed large portions. At home that doesn't happen and also, if you don't understand something you have all the extra time to go over it until you do.

My husband agreed that we could continue with homeschooling after the first year. He eventually told his family and friends. I have to say, he didn't just tell them, he would tell them how marvellous it was and how great this option is and that the girls were doing brilliantly! In the second year he let the girls come to his business and didn't mind telling customers that they are homeschooled. I am actually shocked at how much his view has changed in such a short time. I honestly thought I would have a battle on my hands every year, but now he doesn't question us and lets me take control. He still doesn't help to homeschool them, it is all left to me - that was part of his original deal too - but to be honest, I prefer it that way.

This past year I also had the chance to prove to him that I shouldn't have any problems getting the girls to sit their end of schooling exams (IGCSE/GCSE). My son had wanted to take the option of studying French at school but the school said there wasn't enough interest and only Spanish could be taken. He had spent three years studying it at school and now they wouldn't let him finish! My son was so upset and I knew he could do it. Knowing the exam system for homeschoolers, I approached the school and asked that if he could he sit the exams in the school and have assignments marked by the school's French teacher, if I taught him French at home. The school agreed as they knew he was capable. So I taught my son French at home, following the curriculum but doing it in my own way as he preferred - an option not available in school. The school marked his assignments and entered him for his exam. He passed with a grade A. So now I feel so much more confident in myself and it also proved again to my husband that homeschooling does work!

Karima is a homeschooling mum of three from the UK. She enjoys spending time with her family and doing anything craft related which she loves sharing on her blog karimascrafts.com

A Guide To Getting Started

By Umm Ibrahim Samirah

So you've decided that homeschooling is for you (or at least that you want or need to give it a try). You're probably feeling overwhelmed and/or confused as to what your next steps should be (been there, done that). In many ways, you are fortunate because there is a wealth of information out there. When I started homeschooling, there were just a handful of sites that offered advice and information on homeschooling; the opposite is thankfully true today, alhamdulillah. I've been asked various questions over the years regarding how to get started, so I thought I'd throw my hat into the ring as well.

Below I outline a series of steps for getting started with homeschooling. Except for the first step (which you may have done already), you could really do them in any other order. I just enumerated them by what was a logical sequence to me. You may want to get a notebook or even a binder (probably better) started because during this endeavor to get started, you'll come across a lot of information and you want to stay organized so that you can refer back to that information as needed. (Organization is a skill you will definitely want to try to master during homeschooling, trust me).

1. Check homeschooling requirements for your locale

States and provinces differ on their homeschooling requirements but it is usually on this level that you want to start looking for information as to what is expected of you. In some states, like mine, you must register as a private school to homeschool independently; in others you may simply have to register as a homeschool. Some states require portfolios and attendance records to be submitted regularly throughout the year, some don't. In some states you may have to meet with a teacher. You should be able to find out what is expected of you as a homeschooler, by visiting your state's Department of Education website. In other countries, these are sometimes called the Ministry of Education. You can google "state education departments" or stop.by this site which currently has links to each state's education department websites: bit.ly/1oHRd68

Binder Tip: You may want to set up a tab/divider with this information in your binder - perhaps labeled "Legal Requirements" so you can refer to it when you need it. For my state, you have to fill out an affidavit with your school information so this is a handy place to keep a copy of it.

2. Find out what you should teach

Once you know what is expected of you legally as far as homeschooling, the next thought that probably comes to mind is "What should I be teaching?" Well, you are the educator, principal and superintendent of your homeschool, so in essence you have control over what you will teach. Some states require certain subjects to be taught, so you'll probably want to begin this portion of the search back at your state education department if you didn't already come across this information.

The typical core courses for education are: math, English, social studies, and science. In high school, students will also take electives and in lower grades, art and programming are common extra classes. You could add sewing, home economics, religious studies, etc. One resource that has been very valuable over the years for me in deciding what specifically to teach, is the World Book's Course of Study section where it not only lists the typical classes taken per grade, but also lists "standards," that is, specific topics and skills or expectations for a given grade level (Preschool to Grade 12). Other resources that I have used to see what is generally taught at different grade levels are online table of contents of textbooks.

A quick word about grade levels:
In the course of homeschooling, you may very well find that your student is on grade level for his/her age in some topics and behind or ahead of grade level in others. This is very normal in homeschooling. SimpleHomeschool.net has a great article on "Stepping Outside the Grade Level" which I highly recommend you read. (bit.ly/1oHRo1l). The best approach is to tailor your homeschool curriculum toward each individual child. If he/she would be in 4th grade, but needs 5th grade English or 3rd grade math, then that's what you should give him or her. You can use traditional grade levels as a starting guide, but don't feel bound to them. As *The Homescholar* put it:
"Focus on providing a curriculum that is challenging and not overwhelming. Be sure to keep it academically rigorous and encourage them to do their best, but guard against burnout and overwork that can lead to frustration."

One beauty of homeschooling is that you can choose the materials to accurately match your student's level in each subject.

Binder Tip: Label a section of your Binder, "Course of Study" and put the information from this portion of your homeschool search in that section. When you have definitively chosen your subjects, you may want to fill out/make a Course of Study form (DonnaYoung.org has some great ones) which list the courses for a given year as well as the books/resources you will use.

Now as I said, the next steps do not have to necessarily be undertaken in the steps outlined below. Maybe for you, not all are necessary.

3. Discover your child's learning style
If you have more than one child, I'm sure you have realized that they each have their own strengths, weaknesses, and interests. One advantage of homeschooling is that you can pick curriculum or teaching methods that fit each child. Some children may do better with a hands on learning approach while another child may learn better through listening. As with anything, you can google and find inventories, quizzes/tests or simply articles to read. To help you get started, I offer a list of some below:

- How to Homeschool: Determine Your Child's Learning Style: http://bit.ly/1KVBBXc
- Homeschool.com's Learning Style Quiz: : bit.ly/1L5tEaK
- Six Tools to Find Out Your Child's Learning Style: bit.ly/1b0HQ7Q
- Homeschooling Toddlers to Tweens - Know Your Students: bit.ly/21txB7K
- Learning Styles Inventory - Find Your Child's Learning Style: bit.ly/1Qnhyh8

Binder Tip: You may want to have a section for each student in your binder and keep information like this in that section for a specific student or you may have a section labeled "Learning Styles" and keep all of this information for all kids handy there.

4. Explore homeschooling methods and approaches

So you think you are ready to start picking curriculum? Well, you can, but you should know (if you already don't) that in homeschooling there are many approaches and philosophies and being familiar with them (as well as your child's learning style) can help give you direction for your homeschooling as well as aid you in selecting a curriculum that is a good fit for your child. Among the homeschooling approaches, these are among the most popular:

School at home

You use traditional school textbooks, you set a typical public school like schedule - essentially you replicate school at home. This approach is what many homeschoolers typically start off with because it's what they know. For some homeschoolers, this works and they stick with it throughout their homeschooling journey. But for perhaps the majority of homeschoolers (or at least a good portion), they quickly (or may eventually) find that this brings about too much stress for mom or dad and the kids. If it works for you, that's awesome. But if it doesn't, don't be alarmed. Try something different. And that's how researching the different methods now, can help.

Among the other methods:
Computer Based/Charter School Learning
Classical Education
Charlotte Mason
Waldorf
Montessori
Unit Studies
Eclectic
Unschooling
and there are others.....

Other homeschoolers have written more eloquently than I probably can on these methods, so these are some resources where you can learn about these approaches as well as other approaches or methods of homeschooling:

- Homeschool.com's Homeschool Approaches: www.homeschool.com/Approaches
- Choosing a Homeschooling Method: Which One is Right For You?: bit.ly/1TK3cfc
- Homeschool Diner's Guide to Homeschool Approaches (this one's really good!): bit.ly/1oSeOSm
- Homeschool 101: Methods and Styles: bit.ly/1TMgRDW
- Methods and Styles of Homeschooling: bit.ly/1LpGqIa

5. Select a curriculum

One of the biggest parts of homeschooling is, of course, choosing your curriculum. The original definition of *curriculum* is actually just the subjects and courses taken. In homeschooling, it has come to mean the resources that you will use to teach. Keep in mind though that *curriculum* does not just mean textbooks. There are so many options when it comes to homeschooling curriculum, it can be overwhelming. Here's a brief look at different types of curriculum, there are many more.

Out of the box/full curriculum
Many companies offer a full curriculum already set up for you, based upon the grade level of your child. These tend to be very costly for a great many homeschoolers. But if you have the money and/or you want to have everything already planned out for you, this may be an option. An example of this would be BookShark.

Distance learning
This is where you homeschool through a program that typically sends you the books and materials you need (sometimes the materials can be accessed online). Some may offer teacher services where you are assigned a teacher to help you grade/teach or advise.

- Oak Meadow
- Calvert Education

These can be costly as well, but there are more affordable or free options available. A much more affordable option includes programs such as Time4Learning, which is totally computer based and it keeps records/track of your student's learning (though it does not offer high school diplomas). the cost is approximately 20 USD dollars per month.

There are free options as well, which technically fall under public charter schools. Some examples of these include:
- K12
- Connections Academy

We have used these two programs in the past. They provide all the textbooks for free and have an online interface where students access lesson plans, lessons, and take tests and quizzes. Work samples are required to be submitted on a regular basis and you are assigned a teacher that you must meet with typically once a month to turn in work. Students (typically grades 2/3 and up) are required to sit for standardized testing in the spring of each year.

Local charter public homeschool options
My family discovered these a few years ago. They are basically the same thing as K12 and Connections Academy, however there is a local brick and mortar charter school where you meet monthly with an assigned teacher to submit work. They provide the textbooks for free and tuition is free as well.

I am not familiar with other states, but some examples of this (in California) are:
- Learn4Life.org
- iLeadExploration - this is the school we will be schooling through this year, insha Allah. It is available in Los Angeles, Orange, San Bernardino, Kern and Ventura counties in California. In this program, the parent gets to select the curriculum. Many of the other public homeschool program typically just use public school textbooks.

These can be nice options if you can't afford a lot of textbooks or want/need some guidance.

Put together your own curriculum
Instead of buying a full curriculum, you can pick and choose your resources for each class on your own. There are hundreds of homeschooling companies that offer homeschool curriculum. An example of a company that offers homeschooling resources is Rainbow Resource which is very popular as it has such a comprehensive selection and the prices tend to be cheaper than other sites.

For most of our homeschooling, however, I never really purchased textbooks or materials. For 10 years, we lived overseas and had no way of receiving mail (or in some cases it was just too costly), so I put together my own curriculum through free textbooks, workbooks, and lessons that I found online. In addition, I have made a lot of my own resources (lessons, worksheets) as well.

When putting together your curriculum, don't forget to look beyond textbooks. You can find online lessons, such as the video lessons from Khan Academy, which are free. You can find PowerPoints such as those at Pete's PowerPoint Station.

When I started homeschooling, there were not so many resources for homeschooling. Now, the choices are staggering. And many are free. If purchasing a curriculum is not really an option for you, look to the internet and even your local library which may have textbooks that you can check out. In our early days of homeschooling, we discovered a "book bank" which offered thousands of old school books from public schools for free, so look around for those as well.

6. Organizing your homeschool and creating study spaces
Organizing your house
Point blank - It's hard to homeschool in a messy, unorganized home. That's just reality. And you may find that while homeschooling, your house is never up to the level of cleanliness that you think it should be. That's also reality. But everything that you can do to get your household running smoothly will go a long way. So, if you haven't already, set up chore schedules and laundry schedules, and get rid of junk.

Organizing your days
Now, I'm not just talking about school day schedules. I'm talking about your whole day. Schooling is just one aspect of your day. The rest of your life makes up the rest of the hours and you'll want to get it organized. In turn, that can help your school day run more smoothly, in sha Allah.

I recommend starting with two things to organize your day:
For Muslims, start with the prayer times and build everything else around it. If your children are too young to pray, well, you've still got to pray. Establishing "break times" around the prayers will help you get your prayers in and help older kids establish the prayers.

Secondly, establish morning and evening routines. You don't want your kids to just get out of bed and "do school." They've got to eat, groom themselves, and help out with chores to keep the house running more smoothly. Build these routines first (and then be diligent about your kids following them until they become second nature).

Organize your school year and days
Start off by defining your school year. Will you homeschool all year round? Will you homeschool

the traditional nine months and break for the summer? Some homeschoolers homeschool all year round and then take a week break every 4, 6, or 8 weeks, for example. This method worked well for us because in the beginning, I didn't schedule any breaks and we would get burnt out and take an impromptu break (which is not necessarily bad). But I found that working hard for x weeks and taking a scheduled break was very motivating and perhaps lead to less burnout, *Allahualim*. Google examples of different homeschool schedules. Don't forget to include holidays as days off in your schedule if you observe them. Muslim homeschoolers typically take off days for Eid and Ramadan and you could also take off voluntary fasting days such as Yawmul Asharah or Yawmul Arafah to encourage fasting and provide a short break. Once you decide, it's a good idea to draw up a yearly calendar and distribute it to your kids (and post it on a wall as well) so they can know what to expect.

Define your weeks and days

There are many ways you can structure the school days and weeks. Some school for the traditional Monday - Friday. Some school for four days (Monday - Thursday) and have Fridays off. Some school over the weekend and leave a work week day or two off so errands can be run without interrupting the school day or so that field trips can be taken when places are open. Define your work week. Again, you can start off with the traditional school week and tweak it as you see what actually falls into place for your family.

For your days, you can use a traditional school day schedule, with specific time periods for each subject everyday. You can do block scheduling where you set up chunks of the day (a morning session and an afternoon session, for example). You might choose to only do certain subjects on certain days of the week or study science this week and social studies the next. You have that flexibility. You don't have to do all classes everyday (though most feel good about keeping math and English daily). When I started homeschooling, most resources I read said to get math and English or more stringent subjects out of the way in the morning and save the afternoon for lighter subjects and projects. But sometimes the afternoon seemed great for math for some of my kids whereas for others, it was best to start the day with it.

And how many hours should you homeschool? Some people spend all day homeschooling. Some only spend the mornings. You might start off with a traditional schedule and then gradually make changes as you see fit. You can surf online for examples of school day schedules. Once you've got a schedule in mind, write it down on paper and share it with the kids. You may also find that the schedule you keep depends on the curriculum you choose, so if you set up a schedule later but find that it won't work for your curriculum, you may need to tweak it at that time. And, although it may be easier (for you) to keep all the kids on one schedule, doing the same subjects at one time, in reality, it might not work out so well for the kids (some might finish way ahead of the allotted stop time, some may still be working at the cutoff and need a great deal more time). Flexibility is key in homeschooling, you've got to try to balance between what is good for the kids and what you are able to deal with as well.

Organizing your study space(s)

Notice I didn't say homeschool classroom? Many homeschoolers have a dedicated room for homeschooling, like a classroom. Some have a dedicated area of a room (such as the dining table or a corner) for a study area. Some have, well, neither. Sometimes we've had a schoolroom or area, sometimes my kids have studied in their rooms, sometimes my kids have studied in my room. My husband believes that sitting at a table or desk is the best. In my experience, the best has turned out to be sometimes on my bed with several kids surrounding me so I can help them as needed. You might start out with desks or using a table but find that for some of your kids, lying on their bed studying works for them. And, don't be alarmed or disheartened when you see all the beautiful homeschool classroom pictures online. If you are able to set up a dedicated room or area that's awesome. But if that's not possible due to finances or space constraints, make do with what you do have/can provide.

I've found some really cute classroom decorations at the Dollar Tree or the 99¢ Store. So if you are on a tight budget, be sure to check those places out. I've found some great calendar wall displays that you might see in a classroom, for example, and they are just a buck! Sometimes you can find places online, such as government agencies or organizations, which will send you posters that you can hang up. And finally, if your finances don't permit, you can find a lot of neat resources from fellow homeschoolers online or make your own! And, there have been times, like now, where I don't have a single chart, calendar, reference chart, etc. up on the wall - but learning still takes place.

Lesson planning
Once you have selected your curriculum, you'll need to plan it out (unless you purchase a curriculum that plans out the days for you). A simple way to plan is to plan for the year by taking a look at your textbooks or resource books, calculate the available days you will have for instruction and divide it by the number of pages or lessons in the book. This method is simple, but sometimes not the most efficient. For example, some concepts may take longer for your student to grasp and you may want to spend more days on a lesson than just one.

Some homeschoolers plan for an entire year at once. Some homeschoolers plan by months, some by weeks, and some day by day. I really don't recommend day by day planning as I did that for many years and it can be very stressful. I suggest planning for the year if you are able to and tweaking as necessary, but if a week ahead is all you can get, well that's something. Preparation is key - as Benjamin Franklin said, "Fail to plan, plan to fail." I've found that to be so true in homeschooling, so as hard as it may be for some, try to conquer that lesson planning. You don't want to wake up each day and just wing it. You need to have some type of goal to work towards (which lesson planning provides). On the other hand, I've fallen prey to over-planning - making up elaborate lessons that were just too grand and didn't get finished because they just weren't practical. When planning your lessons, try to go beyond the textbook with audios, videos, PowerPoints, games, living books, and field trips, but sometimes, doing a lesson right out of the book is ok too.

The beauty of homeschooling is that there is much room for flexibility. So while I suggest planning for the year as much as you are able to, realize that your "year" can be 12 months or 13 or 14... etc. If you are using textbooks, at the very least, see how many lessons you will need to do to complete it and make a list of them and use it as a measure of progress. If you remember your own schooling years, you got a lot of "refreshers" in math and language year after year. So, if your child has mastered a topic, say nouns, there really is no need to keep doing the same type of grammar exercises in nouns, each year. That can save you some time to concentrate on the topics that are more challenging. Make your curriculum fit your student, not the other way around. And, by the way, if you decide to change your curriculum mid-year, know that many others have done that as well.

Homeschooling is a wonderful experience. But it is also a challenging one. You may have some students who will work hard and get their work done and others who are just not interested or motivated and provide a great amount of resistance. In homeschooling, there is truly no one-size-fits-all schedule or curriculum and you have to be flexible, to respond and try something new when what you are doing just isn't working. It's tough, but just because it's tough doesn't mean you can't do it. Some will graduate their homeschoolers. Some will try homeschooling and eventually revert to or turn to public or private schooling or tutoring. The key is to do what you think is right for your kids and don't worry about what others are doing or what they will think.

Phew! Feeling overwhelmed? That's normal. I've been homeschooling for over 18 years and sometimes I still feel overwhelmed or like I am back to square one. If you can find a support group - whether online or in person - that can make a big difference for you. There will be a lot of trial and error. Embrace it. And remember, homeschooling does not have to be school-at-home. If it works for you, great, if not, don't despair. The purpose is to educate our children; yes, we give them knowledge that they can take out into the world and use/apply. But it also includes helping them develop the powers of reasoning, judgement, coping, and other skills to make it as a mature adult. And a lot of that you can't get from books. You get it from life. Don't get so bogged down with homeschooling that you forget to live. Embrace the lazy days where you may not crack open a book but you stop and smell and discuss the roses which leads to a discussion of the beauty of creation and ultimately why we were put on this earth. Or, you decide that you want to try a new recipe and everyone is in the kitchen helping out, getting an impromptu math lesson on fractions, and learning to be a part of a team. Or you read a news article about a recent event and you spend hours discussing it, giving an impromptu lesson in geography and history. This is all education. This is all homeschooling.

Sherrie (aka Umm Ibrahim Samirah) runs the blog TJ Homeschooling (formerly known as Talibiddeen Jr.) She's a homeschooling stay-at-home mom/stepmom of 10. She has been homeschooling since 1998 and has been sharing online resources and printables for homeschooling, as well as for the home and family, since 2002!

This article is reprinted with Umm Ibrahim Samirah's permission. It originally appeared on tjhomeschooling.blogspot.com.

How To Create A Homeschooling Budget

By Ismail Kamdar

The idea of lack of school fees is a major incentive for some parents to begin homeschooling. School fees, especially for private Islamic schools, can be expensive, so it is only natural that one would think that homeschooling is a cheap alternative. While homeschooling is definitely cheaper than sending your child to a private school, there are still many expenses that you need to budget for. First time homeschoolers may be unaware of these expenses and soon find themselves struggling financially or even in debt due to poor planning.

If you are aware of common homeschooling costs, you can easily plan to fit all expenses into your budget. In this article, I will detail some of the common costs associated with homeschooling as well as tips on how to save money and be more frugal.

Start-Up Costs
If it is your first year of homeschooling, your costs will be a bit higher because you will need to budget for start-up costs. These include desks, chairs, and any resources or stationary that you will need. This may also include whiteboards, charts, bookshelves, and science equipment. In some countries, there are registration costs as well.

In my case, we moved to a larger apartment so that we would have an extra room to use as a class, so we included moving costs and higher rent into our budget. If you already have a space that can be utilized for studying then you won't need to worry about that.

Remember that a lot of the things that you will purchase in your first year can be used for many years if you purchase good quality furniture and tools. Don't just look for the cheapest deals, but consider the quality too.

Stationary and Books
Stationary and books are your most common recurring cost. With young children, stationary goes missing or breaks very easily, so you will frequently find yourself needing to purchase new pencils, erasers, sharpeners, pens, and art supplies, perhaps even monthly. You should keep aside money for this in case something goes missing and you need to replace it.

Private Lesson Fees
As you are homeschooling, you will have to pay for private lessons in any extracurricular activity that you can't teach your children yourself. You may find that such lessons can be costly. These

lessons range from sporting activities like soccer, swimming, and martial arts, to artistic interests like painting, drawing, and creative writing. Eventually, your child will want to learn something that you can't teach them.

Private lesson fees might also include Islamic classes, as you may want to hire a private Qur'an instructor or madressa teacher to teach them the basics if you are unable to do so yourself. These fees need to be factored into your monthly costs.

When it comes to such lessons, my advice is to look around for the best deal you can get. The best deal is not necessarily the cheapest, rather it is the best value for your money. Spend sometime looking for someone who offers high quality lessons at affordable fees. You can also save money by enrolling them in a group class, which is generally cheaper than one-on-one private classes.

Family Excursions
Another cost you need to keep in mind is family excursions. You cannot sit at home all day and there will be days when you and your kids would rather visit the local zoo, aquarium, park, or museum instead. These trips tend to be costly for families so it is important to research prices and discount options, and budget accordingly.

Depending how often you make such trips, the amount of money you will need to allocate for this will differ. On average, once a month or once every two months should be enough for a family excursion. Check with venues if they have homeschooling discounts or special annual memberships. Some places that offer teacher discounts will extend those to homeschoolers when asked.

Food Bill
This is something many parents don't think about, but the food bill for homeschooling parents can be higher than for schooled-children. Your kids will be at home all day, every day and they are growing kids who generally have healthy enough appetites, but be aware of kids who may want to frequently snack just because they are home and can. They don't have a school cafeteria to frequent, and will likely be eating lunch at home, while other kids are at school eating cheaper cafeteria meals or sandwiches.

Of course, eating meals at home is far more beneficial for your children, but for budgeting purposes you need to allocate money for this too, because as your kids grow, your grocery bills will as well. If you don't already, now is a good time to start buying in bulk and learning how to properly store and prepare larger quantities of items bought for less money than smaller portions.

Annual and Monthly Budgeting
Preparation is key for anything to go smoothly. For homeschooling, I recommend sitting down with your spouse at the start of the year and working out both the annual and monthly budgets and discussing how you are going to meet your needs. You will need to consider everything including books, stationary, new equipment, fees for extra classes, transportation costs, excursion costs, and emergency costs. Once you have prepared your budget, you will be able to operate within it and insha Allah you will not have too many difficult surprise costs.

Tips and Advice

All of the above mentioned costs can pile up if you are not careful, and this can be overwhelming for parents who were expecting homeschooling to be free or cheap. Preparation is key, but there are other ways to cut costs too.

One way to save money is to utilize as many digital resources as possible. I downloaded a 48-book set of Grade 1 e-readers and used them to teach all my kids to read. This saved me a lot of money compared to purchasing the printed books, and having to replace them anytime one got torn or lost. Digital resources can be a great money saver.

Another way to save money is to re-use whatever can be re-used. With writing books and stationary, this is not possible. However, reading books and activity sheets can be re-used. Regarding activity sheets, there are two ways to make them re-useable. You can either make copies of each sheet, or have your child do it in pencil and then next year, erase that and have the next child use the same sheet.

It is worth investing in a copy-printer as you can save a lot of money by using it to make copies or download and print worksheets. There are innumerous free resources for printables and downloads online. You can also save money by buying bulk supplies of stationary and workbooks. In this way, you will get them at a much cheaper rate, and it will not go to waste because over the years, you will end up using a lot of stationary and books either way. Look for teacher supply outlets both local to you and online. Remember, you are now essentially running a business in your home - a school.

Shaykh Ismail Kamdar is the Head Teacher of Islamic Online University, a BAIS graduate, Radio Presenter, founder of Islamic Self Help, author of multiple e-books and a homeschooling dad.

Learning To Speak Their Language

By Klaudia Khan

Seeing school-age children out and about during school hours in England is a rather unusual sight. The playgrounds are deserted and in the shops you will only meet mummies with babies - there are no children over three years old around. So my family attracts some attention and occasionally people ask: "Aren't they going to school?" When I respond that my children are homeschooled, the next question to follow is some variety of "Why?" And here I don't really know what to say. Not because there isn't a reason for my children to not be going to school, but rather because there are so many reasons it is hard for me to choose one in particular that could explain it all. I often end up saying that they are too young yet, or something along those lines, even though I know fully well that in England even two-year-old babies are eligible for partial nursery, even if they are not toilet trained!

My three daughters are aged five-and-a-half, four and one. The eldest one has just started reading in English and Polish, and reads at least a couple of books every day. I don't mean phonics readers, but proper books, like *Cat in the Hat Comes Back*, which is one of her latest favourites. She is also learning to read in Arabic from a primer and is doing really well, masha Allah. My second daughter has recently discovered writing and covers pages and pages of paper with letters, sometimes writing words that she knows, like her name, and sometimes just random letters, which is fun when I try to read them upon her request. The little one is also learning to write in her own way, making marks with whatever writing equipment she can find on the floor, and on whatever suitable or unsuitable surface she comes across in the house. They are busy and happy playing and learning and it just feels so natural to have them at home with me, learning at their own pace and enjoying their unscheduled playtime. People sometimes ask if it is hard to teach them, but I actually don't do any structured teaching. I answer their questions when they ask me, or if I'm unable to answer them well I search for suitable books to answer them. I read stories and rhymes to them, enjoying it as much as they do, because good children's literature is never 'childish' and can be enjoyed by anyone. I try to inspire them to do some arts and crafts, again by just doing it and hoping they will follow, and generally I act more as a learning facilitator and play companion than a teacher. Children love to learn undisturbed and they do it best that way.

Homeschooling in our home feels natural enough, yet I never planned to do it this way. We were living in Pakistan when my eldest daughter was approaching her fourth birthday, which is the usual school starting age both in Pakistan and in the UK. Her cousins of similar age had already started school and I watched them with pity as they woke up early every morning and hurriedly had their breakfast to catch an old van that collects children from neighbourhoods and transports them to school, often in scary conditions. You can see boys standing on the van's bumper, because it's overcrowded, travelling with good speed on a dual carriageway! So this was my first reason to doubt whether school is the best thing for my children. And then, these kids going to school in Pakistan were not only burdened by the heavy rucksacks (literally), but also by very long school hours, lots of homework and plenty of information to be memorised. I didn't like it at all and decided that if Pakistani schools are like this, then my children would be better off studying at home. I got in touch with some inspiring ladies from a homeschooling group based in Islamabad and slowly the idea of homeschooling as the best form of education seeped into my mind.

Trial schooling
We then moved to the UK and because everyone was praising English schooling so much, I decided to give it a try. The local primary school was within walking distance of us and my daughter got admitted to nursery, where she spent four hours a day playing and learning. She was very shy at first, as she didn't speak any English, only Polish and Pashto, but she learnt to enjoy it and so I thought that maybe school is not so bad in this part of the world. There were some bad things, like all the Christmas, Halloween, and Easter activities, but I decided to overlook them for the time being. Then full-time school started for my daughter, which meant uniforms, strict attendance and very long hours spent at school. She didn't enjoy it anymore.

Seeing her so tired, stressed and unhappy, I decided to take her out of school. This time I had my doubts about my decision; the teachers were saying that she would fall behind in her learning, and our extended family wondered why I was not satisfied with such a good school, they suggested I was jeopardizing her future academic success. It wasn't easy to take the plunge, but the alternative was scary - my daughter's well-being could not be compromised and school clearly made her unhappy. My husband also had his doubts about homeschooling, but I convinced him and myself by saying that it might be just a temporary solution and we could send her back to school when she turns seven years old. Now, a year on, we don't think of school anymore and have managed to shake off the fear of 'jeopardizing future academic success' and other scares that the system tried to feed us.

Finding our style
I am now confident that homeschooling was the right decision and the best option for my children, but making the choice and taking the plunge was not so easy. To begin with, I didn't know how to do homeschooling at all. I bought plenty of workbooks following the English curriculum, phonic readers and flash cards, and I tried to give my daughter a scheduled learning time every day. It didn't work. I was so enthusiastic about the brilliant writing exercises I found and I wanted to share them with her. She was not interested. I tried to explain to her how sometimes two letters join to make one sound, to make reading easier for her. She wouldn't listen. I was getting frustrated and so was she, but Alhamdulillah I decided to just abandon my great big teaching plan and let her be. I remembered that I went to school at the age of seven, and before that no one ever bothered me with phonics or additions, so why should I do it to my girl?

I did my research and found out that English children begin school earlier than other children in Europe and spend the most time there, but this does not really result in better academic performance. They learn to read at a very early age, but most of them never read for pleasure. The situation in some Asian countries is even worse with children spending literally full days at school memorizing tons of often useless information. Then there are constant tests and assessments starting at very early ages and putting a huge pressure on small children. On the other hand, in countries which have seemingly more relaxed approaches to schooling, like the Scandinavian countries or my home country of Poland, (where children start school at the age of seven, spend less hours at school, have longer holidays and less homework), children are performing better academically. I also came across the quote by Ali ibn Abu Talib (RA) who supposedly said that you should play with your children until they are seven years old, then teach them for the next seven years, and befriend them for the next seven years. Now I can breathe with relief. And my children do too.

From that moment I decided that I will only teach my children when they showed an interest in being taught and I will keep it this way until they are seven years old. My method still needed perfecting though, as I could clearly see that they are not very good at following instructions and dislike being questioned or checked in any way, even seemingly playful ways. I thought it was time that I do some proper reading and find out about the different homeschooling methods. The first on my reading list was John Holt's book *How Children Learn*. It was a real breakthrough for me.

Holt advocates that children have an innate drive to learn and if we just let them explore, discover and learn in their surrounding world at their own pace and in their own way, they will learn. They will learn everything that is important for them, everything that is part of life for their families and communities. It may exclude standardized information such as multiplication tables, but it will probably include less measurable knowledge such as navigating social interactions and emotional intelligence. If children have a passion for something - a particular sport, trains, castles, dinosaurs or whatever else - we should let them pursue it and actively support it by providing interesting books, toys and field trips. We should, however, never press them to read anything or play any particular game. We should even restrain ourselves from prompting them like: "Have you read this new book about dinosaurs yet?" This is actually the best way to discourage them from opening it. And, following Holt's methods, we should never attempt to test their knowledge or skills, but rather relax and wait for them to show us. It is hard to begin with, to abandon the idea of curriculum and assessments, but letting go of 'the school within' has really benefitted me, as a homeschooling mother, and my children.

As I let my children run wild in terms of their early education, I can see the great results of it. My eldest daughter loves books, and the youngest ones naturally copy her and 'read' the pictures of whatever she is reading in English or Polish. They keep diaries for a few days at a time and love to write letters, but they would never come near a handwriting exercise book, which I have getting dusty on the shelf. I don't test them in any way to check their progress, but it shines through, especially through the questions they ask and in normal everyday conversations.

There is one exception to Holt's method in our homeschooling: tajweed classes. Three days a week I drive my girls to a tajweed lesson which takes place in a private home, where a group of young students aged three to eight learn with a teacher. They read their lesson for the day and then they are supposed to revise it at home. I do remind them of it, but never force them to do it, and have found that they are most likely to open their Arabic readers when they see my revising my own lesson for my tajweed class. My middle daughter actually learned to read the Arabic alphabet before she learnt the English/Polish one. And because they are exposed to so many different languages - Polish with me; Pashto with their father and cousins living locally; English at playgroup, in books and on selected TV cartoons; and Arabic at madressa - they are now very comfortable switching when speaking to different persons. They work as translators between their maternal grandmother and father and know that one letter can be read in different ways depending on the language it is being used in. They also love to discover new fun words in other languages and take pleasure in discovering how some words may resemble each other in different languages, like when they hear Urdu and find similarities to Pashto or watch *Krtek* – a cartoon in Czech language and try to make out the meaning based on is similarity to Polish.

This is only the beginning of *why* my children are being homeschooled. The list is not complete, of course, as I didn't write anything about prioritising Islamic learning - which is important and only really doable in a home setting. Nor did I mention the idea of attachment parenting - the theory according to which the more attached the children are to their parents at young ages, the more independent they become as they grow older, because they grow up to be confident and feel secure in their environment. I could make this list of why's quite long, but I just don't feel I need to. I am convinced already that homeschooling is the best choice for my family.

Klaudia Khan is a Muslim mum and writer living in Yorkshire, UK. She has three homeschooled daughters and loves to learn, create and play with them.

A Teen's Mid-Education Mindshift

By Iqra Arfeen

Peer pressure, social networking, movies, music and bullying are just some of the things I fell into during my few years at secondary school. These are common problems which most teenagers face in today's society. As the prophet Muhammad (SAW) said: "A good friend and a bad friend are like a perfume-seller and a blacksmith…"

I am fifteen years old, currently being homeschooled and I'm going to sit my GCSE exams this summer. My short journey of secondary school started out when I was in year eight and finished in year ten. In this short time I had become a different person - one who even I didn't recognise at times.

It was mostly peer influence and my own curiosity, as they say curiosity kills the cat. My friends were becoming closer to me, my home was becoming like a B&B - as I only had breakfast, dinner and slept there, and had no communication with my loved ones. But most importantly I was losing a very special connection - one which couldn't be replaced, it was one with the Lord of the worlds. I was missing prayers and constantly felt as though something was missing. I was lost.

During the summer holidays before my third year at secondary school, my parents had decided that it was time to take some action. I was practically failing at school: low grades, more detentions and not giving homework in on time - and sometimes not at all. My parents thought home-schooling would be best for me. My five younger siblings were also getting home-schooled as my mum felt it worked better for them and she thought it would for me, too.

I have to admit, I wasn't keen on the idea at first. My main concern was my friends and that I wouldn't be able to see them any more on a daily basis. I thought that I would eventually lose contact with them, which I wasn't prepared to do. But my parents reassured me by saying that of course I would still be able to see them by planning things with them and calling or texting them. I still wasn't convinced. My parents and I then decided to do some research on home-schooling for GCSE students. We checked a few websites and the majority of the reviews on all of them were positive: students getting a grade of B or higher in their exams and parents being very happy with the service provided.

I started doing some more research on my own about how home-schooling students progressed and where they ended after secondary school. Once again, all was positive.
While doing this research I found a quote by Raymond S. Moore which has stuck

in my mind for a long time and really does apply to me now, "More of family and less of school, more of parents and less of peers, more creative freedom and less formal lessons." I was beginning to warm up to the idea of homeschooling. But, still in the back of my mind I had doubt. My mum advised me to do istakarah, saying it would help me decide and put me at ease. And like she said, istakarah did put me at ease and I was happy with the decision my parents made.

Soon enough the summer break was over and I was about to begin my homeschooling journey. As days went on, I started to feel that this was the thing which had been missing from my life. That one piece of the jigsaw was now in its place. Being at home has many benefits, one of which is that you can pray without being rushed or watched by anyone, except Allah (SWT). I began to start to feel the effects which salah was having in my daily life; I began to feel happier and lighter, no pressure from school and I was able to start to rebuild my connection with my family and most importantly with Allah.

I am currently preparing for my GCSE - which I have spread throughout the year, meaning I will be doing some in the beginning of the year (May/June) and some at the end of the year (October/November). That is one of the many benefits of homeschooling, you are able to choose when and what subjects you want to do. For example, I am just doing biology out of the three sciences as it is the only one I need to do for my future studies and it will get me into a good sixth form, insha Allah.

I am happy and content, alhamdulillah, as I have a little of everything. I'm still talking to and seeing all my friends, but I have also regained my connections with my family and Allah, Alhamdulillah. And I am up to date and enjoying my studies.

If I may, I would like to give some humble advice to anyone in a similar situation - struggling - at school, whether through bullying, peer pressure or just not being able to fit in. Never cut the tie that keeps you connected to Allah. It is the only thing which will help you to get through any difficult situation you are in. Allah is always there and can hear you at any time and wherever you are. He is the only one whom you can trust and always rely on when you need someone to talk to.

Homeschooling has definitely been a turning point for me in my life, education has become very important to me and it is a very important issue in Islam, too. The Prophet Muhammad (SAW) said: "Seeking knowledge is a religious obligation for every muslim (male and female)." *(Ibn Majah)*

Iqra Arfeen is 15 years old, the eldest of six: five girls and one boy. She is a homeschooling student and sitting exams this year insha Allah. She has many hobbies, some of which are reading, spending time with friends and family, baking/cooking and playing Xbox. She also has a passion for writing, whether it be stories or articles.

From Bullied To Blossoming

By Isra Ali

In September 2012, I began my first day of secondary school. I was really excited to meet different students, see new teachers and above all make new friends. My morning was going great until I entered my new class and saw someone from my primary school who used to bully me. My fear of school rose again and all of the bad memories, of me being bullied, came back. I am 15 years old. Bullying is a topic that is very dear to my heart and I would like to share my journey through this tough time with you.

I have been a victim of bullying since the age of 10, which then occurred continuously for two whole years. The bullying started off with small groups of girls forming in class and me being left out. As I carried on day by day the bullying started to get worse: I would enter class and girls would have already positioned themselves into seats and when I would ask "Who will sit next to me?" they would say "No, we're not sitting next to her, you go…" amongst each other. So, every day of my school life would be like this. At break and lunch times little groups were already formed, again purposely leaving me out.

I realised after a while that they didn't want to be around me because for them I was just a "prissy sensitive girl" who would always talk "cr*p…" - according to two girls in my class. I wasn't someone who always spoke about boy bands, and music and movies and trash talk, which was dirty joking just so a bit of laughing would happen. This was daily behaviour. On the contrary, I was someone who was honest and would try to tell them that what they were talking about was wrong. I would also tell the teachers if I was upset, but all the girls would insist: "She is too sensitive and weak." I was a goody two shoes to them.

Another sad thing was that teachers never understood what I was going through. Eventually it led me to feel betrayed and to an extent even bullied by teachers' comments. I was told by one unempathetic teacher to *grow up…*

I started to believe I was in the wrong and that there was no point in fighting anymore. I wouldn't be heard, instead I would be blamed. I felt as if I was a burden upon the teachers. So I tried to become a part of the groups and started to do all the things they wanted me to. I started to give importance to things that were never really important in my life. I was becoming someone I never was before and never wanted to be.

After various events kept happening, I slowly started to hate school. My days were never happy. I was nervous all the time and never felt like I was a part of my class. I knew that they would never accept me no matter what I did, they put on a friendly act on in front of teachers, and talked behind my back once the teachers would leave, using me as a scapegoat as and when they wanted to. Eventually cyberbullying started to take place too, so I wasn't even left alone when I would get home.

This wasn't what I wanted, it wasn't a place I wanted to be in, it wasn't what I imagined classmates and teachers to be like. All of this led to behavioural changes. I was constantly crying when I was alone in my room, thinking about the way I was treated. I had many mood swings around my family. It led me to stop eating well, and those words, faces, attitudes, bitterness, lying and betrayal from the girls were always with me. It was slowly eating me up.

After having regular conversations with my parents about my issues at school and being bullied, I decided to ask Allah (SWT) to help me make a decision as to what I should do with my education. The following day I woke up and decided that the best thing for me to do is to get homeschooled. This seemed like my only option. I was a little shaky and a bit hesitant to go forward with such a thing, still it felt like it was the right thing to do.

January 10th 2014 was my last day at school and I was so happy! I knew that by being homeschooled all my troubles would be put to an end, and that by being at home I would feel stress free. Now with Allah's mercy I enjoy being homeschooled with all my siblings and not being pressurised by fellow peers and teachers.

I would like to humbly advise those who experience any form of bullying to never feel you cannot talk to anyone. Always maintain a loving relationship with your loved ones with whom you can open up and tell your worries to, and first and foremost build a relationship with Allah (SWT) who is your Creator and knows you better than anyone, because if "He brings you to it, He will bring you through it." And as Allah so beautifully says in the Qur'an, "Verily after every hardship comes ease" (94:5).

I pray to Allah (SWT) that whoever is experiencing any form of bullying, may Allah give you the strength and ability to make the right decisions and get you through it with His help and from the help of your loved ones. Ameen. X

Isra Ali is 15 years old, a homeschooling student in year 10 currently studying for GCSE. She has five siblings, loves to cook, and write articles for various magazines in her spare time.

Chapter 2
THE FUNDAMENTALS

Designing Your Family Culture

By Chantal Blake

Every family has a culture - inherited or acquired, homogeneous or hybrid. It shapes the way we interact with the world and the people around us. The holidays we observe, the rituals we uphold, and the principles that govern our interactions are all a part of our culture. Through culture, we transmit our values, priorities, and beliefs to our children, which sets the stage for the way our children learn and value learning.

Before establishing our family culture, we must first become aware of it. By reflecting on the family we grew up in, we can look for similarities or differences in the way our home feels, the rhythms that constitute our day, and the traditions that are habituated in our lives. Even if you grew up in a dysfunctional, irreligious, or even abusive family culture, it's important to connect the lines between your experienced past, observed present, and desired future.

Subconsciously, we may find ourselves imitating or recreating the home lives of our childhoods, so awareness is warranted to avoid passing on undesirable cultural traits. To filter through the sum total of cultural influences - whether national, religious, societal, or ideological - you first need to articulate your family's goals. Who do we want to be? If Islam is a central part of your family's identity, as opposed to a cultural coincidence, then the Holy Qur'an offers us a variety of lofty aspirations to build our spiritual, personal, and communal lives. More concretely, instruction for how to worship, greet others, manage our time, conduct business, interact with our spouse and children, etc. can be elucidated by the illustrious example of our beloved Prophet Muhammad (SAW). Of particular importance in our families are the examples of gentle, respectful, and virtuous interactions with children; loving, cooperative, and dutiful interactions with our spouse; and welcoming, personable, and compassionate interactions with our families, friends, and neighbors.

If you're currently in a two-parent household, both you and your spouse can begin the conversation about your family vision and how your current beliefs, views, and habits can support that vision. Discipline, conflict resolution, and media use can be particularly sensitive issues to discuss but imperative in the conversation of childrearing. Don't be afraid to consult with other families, leaders, or professionals to weigh in on these issues.

Naturally, praiseworthy characteristics are best nurtured in a peaceful, stable, and predictable environment. Whether large or small, rented or owned, our homes can be a grounding place for our hearts. Your family's ability to thrive in an urban apartment, beachside yurt, or a house on the hill depends on its members and goals. Choosing where and how you live, how you earn a living, your spending priorities and general financial responsibility can significantly help or hinder the achievement of your family's goals.

The more tangible aspects of cultures like daily rituals, seasonal celebrations, and traditional customs should not be taken for granted. For young children especially, anticipating the day's flow can have a calming effect and reduce the anxiety of unpredictability. This does not have to mean engineering your day to progress like clockwork, but a guided sequence of events and consistent expectations can streamline the day's activities. In homeschooling, we have a great opportunity to tailor our daily rhythm to our family's needs for play, work, quietude, etc., as opposed to living by a calculated timetable.

The holidays and family events that you look forward to punctuate the passing of time and add variety to the months and years. Our bi-annual Eid holidays should be significant to every Muslim family but don't be afraid to add your unique family's fingerprint. Pancake brunches, hiking trips, or community service can be fun ways to cement the connection in your household. All of these cultural events are invaluable opportunities to connect your family to each other, impart your morals and values, and cultivate identity formation.

If you don't know where to begin in understanding or formulating your family culture, start by asking yourself and spouse the following questions*:

1. What do you like most about your children?
2. What are your goals? What would your life look like if things were better?
3. What are your goals for your children?
4. What are your biggest accomplishments?
5. What makes you happy or brings you peace?
6. What are your favorite family memories?
7. What are your best qualities as a parent?
8. What are your family's special rules?
9. Who are your friends? Who do you call when you need help or want to talk? Who do you consider supportive?
10. How does your family have fun? What do you all enjoy doing together?
11. What traditions or cultural events do you participate in and how?
12. What special values or beliefs have you learned from your parents or others?
13. Are you connected to a faith community? Do you worship? How?
14. What is the role of faith in your life? Is faith nurtured in your family? How?
15. How do you see each family member's role?
16. How does your family respond to conflict or disagreements?
17. What are your family's values?
18. How do you invest your time and money?
19. How would you describe your spending habits?
20. How does your home "feel"?

21. How do you interact with guests and neighbors?
22. What are your family's eating and mealtime habits?
23. How does your family use media (digital, visual, literary, social, etc.)?
24. How does your family seek and obtain information?
25. How does your family spend time together on a daily and weekly basis?
26. What are your vacations and holidays like?
27. How do your children feel in your company?
28. Where would your family ideally like to live?
29. If your family had a blog, business, or website, what would it be about and look like?
30. If you gained or lost a significant amount of money, if and how would your family dynamic change?

One of the most satisfying results of a healthy family culture is seeing your lifestyle aligned with your views and values. A general sense of enjoyment, contentment, and peace can abound when the core of your nest is understood and honored. While Islam offers some very clear guidelines on morality, family culture is a great way to articulate how your family negotiates the grey areas of personal opinion and different perspectives. Invariably, our children will see others functioning and behaving unlike ourselves. After clarifying the non-negotiable limits of right and wrong, we can also offer the power of "we". "We don't" or "We do" can affirm your own family culture without necessarily judging or confronting others.

The best aspect of culture is that it is ever-evolving and can't exist without context. Don't be afraid to communicate and share what you're passionate about to your children. Your love for Qur'an, crafts, travel, or astronomy can lay a learning foundation for your home, but your children's own interests should be folded in too. Some people distance themselves from their cultural past, but be mindful of not totally erasing your unique heritage. Take the best of what you've been given and be bold in assimilating new ways and understandings. Circumstances, opportunities, and interests change in ways that challenge us to keep our culture real and relevant. What you've done is not what you always have to do and this gracious space is especially needed in families with varied cultural backgrounds and perspectives. Your grandparents' culture may not translate well to your current situation, so bring your family together to sift through the best of your heritage, environment, and ambitions and piece together a collage that everyone can identify with as "ours".

*These questions were formulated after reading Ann Kroeker's article, "What is your Family Culture?", published on July 22, 2008 at annkroeker.com

Chantal Blake is a writer and unschooling mom of two from New York City. She has lived with her family in different countries since 2008 and archives her stories and adventures at WayfaringGreenSoul.com.

Understanding Child's Play
- The Complex Benefits Of Free Play

By Saira Siddiqui

"'Play is often talked about as if it were a relief from serious learning,' he said. 'But for children, play is serious learning.'" -Fred Rogers

Ever since my children were old enough to interact, I've found their play to be remarkable. The kinds of games and role play their little minds create, the way that children who are strangers can meet and almost instantaneously come together on a playground, each seeming to know a set of invisible rules (though technically no one was old enough to read the handbook) is fascinating. Children can create complex play scenarios from sticks, rocks, or a multitude of simple items. Once I found my youngest engrossed in play for hours using only paper clips. Play seems to be an instinctive, highly complex system of interaction, with benefits abounding.

And yet, somehow, the wonder of play seems to get lost as children start to grow. Why is it that some children are able to keep themselves engrossed in play, and others seem to stop knowing how to do it? Is all play created equal? What are some of the benefits of play?

To begin answering these questions we must first examine how we value play. In our society, we look at play as childishness, befitting only the youngest children. As children grow, we place value in other experiences. School, for example, or perhaps more specifically, time spent inside the classroom is given more value than recess. Step inside a kindergarten classroom versus a middle school class and you'll see a distinct difference in how we value play for children of different ages. As children grow into adults, we tend to believe that learning should be more serious business. And even when play is valued, we continue to inject our own adult-initiated ideas into it. We sign children up for organized sports instead of simply letting them play pick-up style games with friends. We enroll them in classes to develop more formal skills.

In his book *Free to Learn* Peter Gray talks about the importance of a specific type of play he refers to as "free play". Gray defines free, or unstructured play, as an experience that is:

1. Self-chosen and self-directed - this, he states, is crucial because the matter of choice is what motivates many of the social benefits that come from play. There is no compulsion in free play, children participate purely for the joy of it, and are also free to quit when they so desire. This contradicts the types of play in which adults inject themselves, often outlining their rules, and expectations.

2. Motivated by means more than ends - the purpose of play is not to achieve some ends, although

that's not to say that there can be no specified result. It simply means that play must be done for play's sake. The process of playing is what is desired, not a final score, a winner or loser, etc.

3. Guided by mental rules - many see free play as a free for all. In actuality, it is always governed by a set of mental rules. If more formal sports or games are played, those rules must be agreed upon and understood by all participants. Moreover, if these rules do not meet the needs of the group, changes can be made as long as everyone agrees to the changes. In all "'free play'", these mental rules are heeded. When children play with blocks they follow along in a manner befitting whatever it is they are trying to construct. When they play chess, they follow more specific rules. In either case, children demonstrate a great deal of self-control in following the hidden rules of play, often putting aside their own needs in order to conform to the expectations of play.

4. Imaginative - play lives in a world between the "real" and "unreal". It is unreal in that it is made up. There is an element of fantasy or role play involved. And yet it is real in that children are actually acting or performing in some way.

5. Conducted in an alert, active, but non-stressed frame of mind - researchers call this place "flow"; when the mind inhabits a place with new, made up rules or constructs (thus needing to stay alert and focused), and yet non-stressed because there are none of the usual consequences that comes with certain behaviors. This is often viewed as a place for great creative expression.

The benefits of Free Play:
1. Respect, empathy, cooperation - "Social play (that is, all play that involves more than one player) is, by its very nature, a continuous exercise in cooperation, attention to one another's needs, and consensual decision-making." *(Gray, p.34)*

When children play, which (according to Gray) must be consensual, they have the choice to leave at any time. Most children want the others to continue in the play as it is in their best interest. In order to keep their playmates satisfied, children learn how to negotiate and attend to the needs of the other children. This social savvy is one of the greatest benefits of social play.

2. Self-Control - it helps children to "accept the twists and turns of fate and make the best of them, rather than complain." *(Gray, p.38)*

If you've ever seen a group of children playing, chances are you'll see them exert more self-control than they do outside of play. My own children will often fall while jumping off of playground equipment, but instead of running to me for a bandaid, when engaged in social play they'll simply stand up, wipe off their clothes, and keep running. Play allows them to place the greater good of the group above their own individual needs.

3. Creativity and problem solving - creating a playful mood or state of mind improves creativity, which in turn improves problem-solving skills.

Studies show that students performed better on multiple problem solving assessments when engaged in playful acts prior to assessing. They were also better equipped to solve logic problem, even at young ages, when a playful mood was simulated beforehand.

Play is not simply a babysitter for our young children. It is a complex experience that fosters creativity and helps us develop socially. Without play, we lose the ability to create and produce new ideas and arts. Indeed, it brings out the very best in us, from our youngest to our oldest. Rather than focus simply on how our children play, let us raise our sights and envision for ourselves a world in which we, too, benefit from play as adults.

"Life must be lived as play." - Plato

Gray, P. (2013). Free to learn: Why unleashing the instinct to play will make our children happier, more self-reliant, and better students for life. New York, NY: Basic Books.

Saira Siddiqui is a freelance writer/online instructor currently pursuing a doctorate in Social Education from the University of Houston. Prior to having children she taught for several years in the public and private sector. When she is not writing for others she enjoys writing for her own blog, ConfessionsofaMuslimMommaholic.com. She currently lives in Texas with her husband and three never-been-schooled children.

We *Can* Homeschool Arabic And Islamic Studies

By Zakiya Mahomed-Kalla

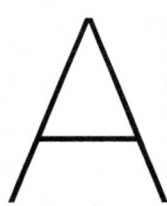rabic and Islamic studies should instinctively be incorporated into a Muslim child's education from early childhood. This is usually done together with secular studies at Muslim/Islamic schools, or at an after school facility. In the homeschooling environment, the challenge has been that parents aren't always equipped to teach Islamic studies and/or Arabic. But today, many families have overcome these obstacles and forged a well-integrated Islamic basis into their homeschooling curriculums.

Teaching Islamic studies at home often seems like a daunting task - what are the subject areas to be taught, what must be included at which phase of a child's learning, and how do we make it interesting and inspiring so that kids want to learn? And then there is often the question of balance - some parents place emphasis on learning Islamic subjects, sometimes at the expense of secular subjects, while others don't consider Islamic studies a significant part of their children's education.

Arabic in the homeschooling environment also appears as too much of a challenge to some parents, who feel they are only able to read Arabic (generally for the purpose of prayer and Qur'an recitation), and can't understand or speak it at all. Sadly, some also do not consider it an imperative subject to fit into their child's homeschooling curriculum.

The Importance of Islamic Studies
Islamic studies is the most pivotal area of learning in a Muslim child's life. And the reward for one who passes on beneficial knowledge, and specifically the Qur'an, is immense.

'Uthman (RA) narrated from the Prophet (SAW): "The best among you (Muslims) are those who learn the Qur'an and teach it." *(Sahih al Bukhari)*

Furthermore, a parent who leaves behind a righteous child leaves behind a legacy that will benefit them in the hereafter. The one who instilled the righteous behaviour (via teaching it) leaves behind another lasting legacy.

'Abdullah bin Abi Qatâdah narrated that his father said: "The Messenger of Allah said: 'The best things that a man can leave behind are three: A righteous son who will pray for him, ongoing charity whose reward will reach him, and knowledge which is acted upon after his death.'"
(Sunan Ibn Majah)

Can I teach Islamic studies to my kids at home?

Islam being the knowledge-rich religion that it is, finds parents often questioning whether they are suitably qualified to take on the responsibility of teaching Islamic studies to their children. Speaking to homeschooling parents who have risen to the challenge, the general result seems to be one of great fulfilment - both for parents and children. The practicality of Islam, and the resulting simplicity of teaching it, and children grasping it by way of example is a beautiful process that parents are discovering every day in homeschooling environments. The very reason that some parents opt for homeschooling in Islamic education in particular, is to move away from the traditional, often rote system of learning the rituals of the faith.

Radio 1584 presenter, and homeschooling parent Rubina Ghoor tells of how she learnt her Islamic basics in a compartmentalised, dogmatic environment, where the focus was on the quantity of information, rather than holistic transformation. Juleika Kalla, home-schooling parent of three has found local Islamic schools sadly lacking in certain areas, and seeks to "instill the love and the ways of the Prophet (SAW) and his companions, and good *akhlaaq* (manners)" herself at home.

In terms of Islamic studies, Muslim parents should at least have the necessary basic Islamic knowledge, if not more, to teach this learning area. Armed with authentic books on fiqh, Islamic history, hadith, and tafseer, and a commitment to improving their own knowledge, parents can certainly cover these with their children. "When you are practising on what you know, Allah increases your knowledge, and when you take that responsibility on, you make a concerted effort to increase your knowledge," explains Umme Uthmaan, home-schooling mother, and Tarbiyyah teacher at Madrasah Riyadhus Saaliheen. If anything, passing on Islamic knowledge can become a beautiful Islamic bonding time between parents and children. When questions regarding specific *masaa'il* (Islamic rules) come up, parents and older children would do well to consult with a local scholar, but more complex questions are only likely to occur as children grow older.

What should be in the curriculum?

Breaking up the curriculum for Islamic studies into manageable subjects for kids is left to the parents discretion. So the question then is, where do we begin?

Teaching duas and fiqh should begin right from when a child learns to speak and do things for himself. Foremost in the duas should be the first kalima, and sleeping and eating duas. Fiqh at this level is very basic, and should start with how to go to sleep in the Prophet's (SAW) way, how to go to the toilet, eating with the right hand, etc. So essentially at this stage, fiqh and duas go hand in hand - as the way of doing things is taught, the duas come in simultaneously.

The teaching of Islamic knowledge between the ages of two to six need not be structured as a sit-down lesson, but rather practically taught when the appropriate occasions arise, on a daily basis. The kalima can be taught over a few nights, as one puts a child to bed for example. This type of incidental learning is practical, and easily absorbed by young minds.

Other Islamic subjects such as *tafseer* (Qur'anic commentary), Islamic history, and *hadith* (the Prophet's sayings and tradition) can be taught when a child is a little older. The Seerah of the Prophet (SAW), and stories of his companions and other illustrious figures in Islamic history can be introduced by way of bedtime stories. The other essential component of Islamic studies is learning to read the Qur'an, and understanding it. This begins from learning to read Arabic alphabets, moves on to alphabet assimilation, reading joint letters with vowels, and finally reading words. A commonly used series for learning to read is *Yassarnal Qur'an*, of which there are different versions, and series across countries. This initial stepping stone in reading should ideally be the simultaneous introduction to the language of the Qur'an and of paradise - Arabic.

Incorporating Islamic studies into secular studies

Islamic studies can be incorporated into secular teaching, to achieve a holistic, time-saving teaching model for parents. When teaching a scientific phenomenon such as the stages of human development in the womb for example, the verses pertaining to this in the Qur'an can be taught simultaneously, as part of the lesson. This teaches children to think Islamically, and not separate Islam and academic thought.

Islamic history can be taught side by side, and related to, world history. Ahaadeeth on eating can be taught together with healthy nutrition, and so forth. Homeschooling mother Umme Uthmaan began reading stories of the companions to her sons, and then used the same books to cover English reading practice, and even grammar rules. This is an excellent example of the overlapping of subject material, and incidental integration that is unique to home-schooling and flexible curriculums. Geography can be introduced with an Islamic slant from a book such as *Muslim Cities Then and Now*, which is part of the *Islamic School Book* range by Goodword Books.

What About Arabic?

Teaching Arabic can be quite the challenge for parents who do not know the language at all. But most parents are able to at least read the language, so they can acquire the basic reading skill books and begin working through these with their kids.

Later on, as more language skill is required, an outside tutor could be called in for lessons. The great opportunity that exists with homeschooling, which is not generally possible in school, is that parents can sit in on these lessons and learn together with their kids.

Where do we begin?

Studies have found that children's ability to absorb and acquire new languages is at its peak between birth and puberty. Moreton First, a division of the UK's well-achieving Moreton Hall school, exposes its pre-schoolers of three years old to four languages, which they grasp with amazing ease. Learning language at this stage happens easily and enjoyably through song, and stories, as well as speaking, even if it is prone to error. Young children have the advantage of not being self-conscious, and will try just about anything that is fun for them.

Parents should be consciously using the language to talk to their children, allowing them to watch videos and listen to nasheeds in Arabic, as well as exposing them to friends their age who are either natives or learning the language, in order to allow their vocabulary and language skill to grow. As mentioned earlier, learning to read the Qur'an is essentially learning to read Arabic. If we build on this initial link between Islamic studies and Qur'an, more links come about naturally. For example, another form of incorporation can take place between Arabic and Islamic studies, whereby children learn Qur'anic vocabulary (by learning the meaning of certain words in their mother tongue) and are then taught to look for them in (simple) ahadeeth, and perhaps later on, Arabic books of fiqh and tafseer, etc.

At a young age, when children are taught duas, it is very beneficial for them to learn the meaning of the duas in their mother tongue. This is another way in which they can gain Arabic vocabulary. As they gain more Arabic vocabulary, the parent or teacher must capitalise on this new-found knowledge by way of constant emphasis, the best of which is speaking.

Besides being the chosen language for the Book of Allah and of paradise, there is another reason why parents and children alike should acquire Arabic - learning additional languages increases critical thinking skills, creativity and flexibility of the mind, according to longitudinal studies by Harvard University. So, Arabic and Islamic studies can certainly be taught via homeschooling, and should be to create a generation of the ummah that knows its roots and understands the religion, on more than one level.

"Allah, this (my children) is what you have entrusted me with, and you would not have entrusted me with it, if I wasn't capable of fulfilling it." - Umme Uthmaan

Zakiya Mahomed-Kalla is an education enthusiast, and an aspiring linguist. She tutors Economics for the University of South Africa, and Arabic for the love of it. Some of her writing is currently on zakiyamahomed.com

Quality Time: Putting 'Home' Back Into Homeschool

By Asma Ali

It's 2 pm and my boys are jumping up and down out of sheer joy, looking at each other in excitement and disbelief. You'd be forgiven for thinking I had just surprised them with an impromptu holiday or given them permission to eat jelly and ice cream for the rest of the week, but the truth is far more plain: I had merely proposed some time out to do a jigsaw puzzle together.

Their unexpected reaction finally caused me to realize what we had been missing.

Quality not quantity
Having moved to Saudi Arabia, my husband and I agreed it would be best for our children to go to a Qur'an school every morning to study hifdh and Arabic. As it would only run from 7 am to 1 pm, I would have ample time to cover other subjects at home and still see and spend good time with the kids outside of academia- hurrah!

Alas, well into the fourth year of part-time homeschooling, I had unintentionally slipped into a methodical (almost mechanical) way of dealing with my children after lunch - we did our Qur'an revision, English, maths, and had some time for reading and outdoor play.

And therein lies the problem: when homeschooling, whether full-time or not, it's easy to assume we are spending plenty of time together as a family simply because the children are at home; we are their prime educators and the ones they are mostly around. But the real question is how much of that time is filled with genuine attention and meaning?

I like to think I make learning fun, but despite spending the majority of their waking hours with me, it was evident my boys needed me to stop being their teacher and start spending quality time with them as their mother.

Reconnecting
It was time for me to pause and reflect on why I had chosen this journey to begin with. I wasn't sure if my children were happy with their busy schooling lifestyle and I most certainly was not convinced that our family life had improved. With a rigid structure in place and self-inflicted pressure for the kids to keep up with secular subjects, I had stopped enjoying our progress and was inadvertently

living the opposite of what I wanted to achieve.

There are several reasons why families may choose to homeschool, but at the forefront of these for many is the advantage of being able to spend more time together. However, amidst the typical days of planning, teaching and running between one activity to the next (not to mention completing chores!) it is easy to forget to appreciate one another's presence and to connect- simply spending time getting to know one another.

Benefits of spending time together
With varying agendas for the day, it can be difficult to find a set time where everyone is available, but incorporating quality time into the routine is essential for the holistic well being of both the parents and their children. Even the smallest of moments together can make a great difference to everyday life and beyond.

Strengthened bonds and relationships
Meaningful interaction is the first step to truly connecting and appreciating every individual. It draws one another closer emotionally and builds on trust in a relationship. Creating this strong bond in the younger years of a child's life will have a positive impact on their psychological and social advancement.

Less behavioral problems
Children love attention from their parents and it is vital to their development. When they don't get enough, many tend to misbehave and cause disruption. Engaging regularly with our kids promotes healthy communication and is proven to counteract negative behaviour. Studies have also shown that teenagers who have open communication with their parents are less likely to be involved with violence and abusive actions in general.

Improved academic performance
Fostering a healthy relationship with our children shows them that they are valued and loved. This enhances self-esteem, which has been associated with greater academic achievement.

Motivation
Spending purposeful time together immediately fills a child with enthusiasm and this actually makes teaching easier and more effective!

What does quality time look like?
My 'jigsaw incident' forced me to pay more attention to how our family was utilizing time together. I was determined to incorporate some quality time into our day and found it's a lot easier to practice than I thought!

Defining quality time and what it looks like varies with every household. While weekends away and regular outings are recognised as clear family bonding time, opportunities to connect are readily available in even mundane tasks, such as housework, as long as we are perceptive and open to them.

I decided to ask some seasoned homeschoolers for their suggestions on simple ideas everyone can weave into their homeschooling days to ensure they're staying connected as a family. The following ten points are just an example of what quality time can look like:

1. Make use of dinnertime
"Dinnertime as a family is essential! We always eat together and talk about life, their day, their dreams, and memories. I never had family meal time growing up and this, for me, is so important to the growth of the family." - *Umm Raiyaan*

2. Have physical contact
"My kids always complain I don't cuddle enough so I try my best to have some close physical contact with each of them everyday. I also recently started staying in bed for half an hour in the morning with the kids watching cooking videos or news I saved from Facebook or Whatsapp." - *Zainab Q.*

3. Read and learn together
"Our quality time is sitting on the sofa just reading a book out loud or sitting round the table learning to draw new things together. It's usually simple, nothing planned. Consciously making an effort to be present and enjoying each other's company is important; just being happy together and smiling, where nothing distracts us." - *Mariya*

4. Let your children choose an activity
"I've recently started playing things with them that they like. Having two boys, alhamdulillah, means a lot of football and Lego, not really my thing but definitely theirs! They like to do this everyday and I join in - just kicking the ball around together, passing, learning new tricks, standing in the goal area. It's only 10-15 minutes, but it makes them so happy!" - *Umm Abdullah*

5. Just play!
"I try to grab the moment when it comes. It could be watching a movie, having breakfast in bed or building a den. Now that we have a baby, I just put a blanket on the floor and lay there as we all play." - *Emmanuelle*

"Just playing with the kids and being funny keeps us bonded. My older ones still like being tickled! We look at old pictures and videos on the laptop and have a laugh at old memories or reminisce. We also have Lego evenings that my husband gets involved in."- *Umm Zakiyyah*

6. Go one on one
"My kids really enjoy some alone time with me, so I stay up with one while the others sleep. Each child likes to talk about different things and I let them lead the conversation. I've learnt a lot about them like this and also ways how they'd like me to improve myself!" - *Bazigha*

7. Party nights
"Mine are getting bigger now and aren't as interested in spending time with us so we have to make a conscious effort. We have a short halaqa followed by a 'party' every night." - *Umm Salam*

8. Watch TV or a film together
"On Friday nights we watch something together, usually a series. Hubby takes the older three bike

riding every Sunday. There are opportunities all the time; it's about being mindful." - *Saffia*

9. Keep open communication and listen
"We talk a lot about our goals as a family, which I feel really helps in keeping us unified. My older ones are girls and they love to just have a chat. We consciously make the effort to connect everything back to Allah in our discussions and give the children reminders naturally without them feeling they are being lectured. This helps them stay connected to their creator and the deen." - *Umm Zakiyyah*

10. Share one another's interests
"As they've got older, my boys just want me to be interested in what interests them, so I try to talk to them about the football league, favourite players, fast cars and sports, etc. Hopefully, if they talk to me about the things that are important to them now, they will still talk to me about the really important things when they are teenagers, inshallah." - *Umm Abdur-Rahman*

Being Mindful
The concept of quality time is something so glaringly obvious, yet it is not given due priority and becomes the first thing we lose in our busy timetables. It's important to remind ourselves to slow down and welcome the shared experience of homeschooling as a family. Cultivating a close relationship with our families helps us bring out the best in each other and creates a loving and nurturing home environment.

Whatever our style is, whether it's following a planned schedule for the day or if we choose to go more free-style, we all need the time to connect. This doesn't necessarily mean taking extra time out to do something together, but focusing on opportunities that are already present in the day. Quality time can happen anytime and anywhere, we just need to be more mindful and aware of our interactions. I can now say on good authority that these precious moments equate to jelly and ice cream everyday! We are in unique positions of being able to watch our children grow, develop and learn. Have fun with it.

"The struggles of today will one day be a distant memory, but your children are only children once. Enjoy them." - Jamerill Stewart

Asma Ali is an avid reader, writer and dreamer who currently resides in KSA where she part-time homeschools her sons.

Peek At A Day
Crayon Resist Art Activitity With Wet-On-Wet Watercolors

By Azra Momin

You will need:
- Crayons or oil pastels • Thick watercolor paper • Watercolors and water • Brushes
- Assorted paper, scissors, glue (optional)

How to do it:

1. Draw designs or patterns on the paper using crayons or oil pastels. You could even write something. Make your lines fairly thick and prominent.

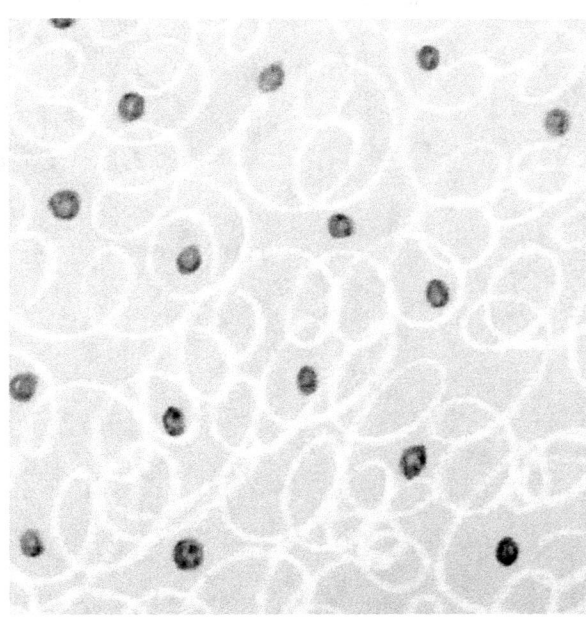

2. Wet your paper with "painting" it with clean water. Now paint with runny watercolor on the wet patches of paper. This is your "wet-on-wet"! The watercolor will not paint over the waxy crayon drawing, because the crayon will "resist" the watercolor (since oil or wax does not mix in water), and your drawing will show through even if you paint over it.

3. Clean your brush between colors, and don't overwork your painting. Keep your colors bright by not overlapping them, or you may end up with a muddy mess. But if that happens, it's OK! Just start over again!

4. Paint the whole paper this way and let it dry. Now you can use it as a base and add more to it. You can use scraps of colored paper (or paint your own) to make pictures to glue on your wet-on-wet sheet, or you can cut out letters of your name and glue those on. Try using the crayons sideways. Try using more than one crayon color in your strokes. Experiment with different types of crayons and oil pastels.

The more you practice wet-on-wet, the easier it will get, and you can start using this technique for more intricate work. Try this: Draw a picture. Wet a small part of that picture, and try wet-on-wet in that small part. Let the colors "bleed" into each other, as shown in the picture below. Complete your whole picture this way. Don't be discouraged by your first attempts, and remember to have fun!

Azra Momin paints, draws pictures for children's stories, and makes textile art and jewelry, not necessarily in that order. She runs process art workshops and is creating an illustrated book about tea. Her favorite time is time spent with her favorite people - her husband and unschooled daughter. Azra enjoys reading mystery novels, and dreams about living in an earth ship. She lives by her motto: No Ordinary Day.

View this tutorial in colour, or see more of Azra's work at www.azramomin.com. You can reach her at azra@azramomin.com for commissions and collaborations.

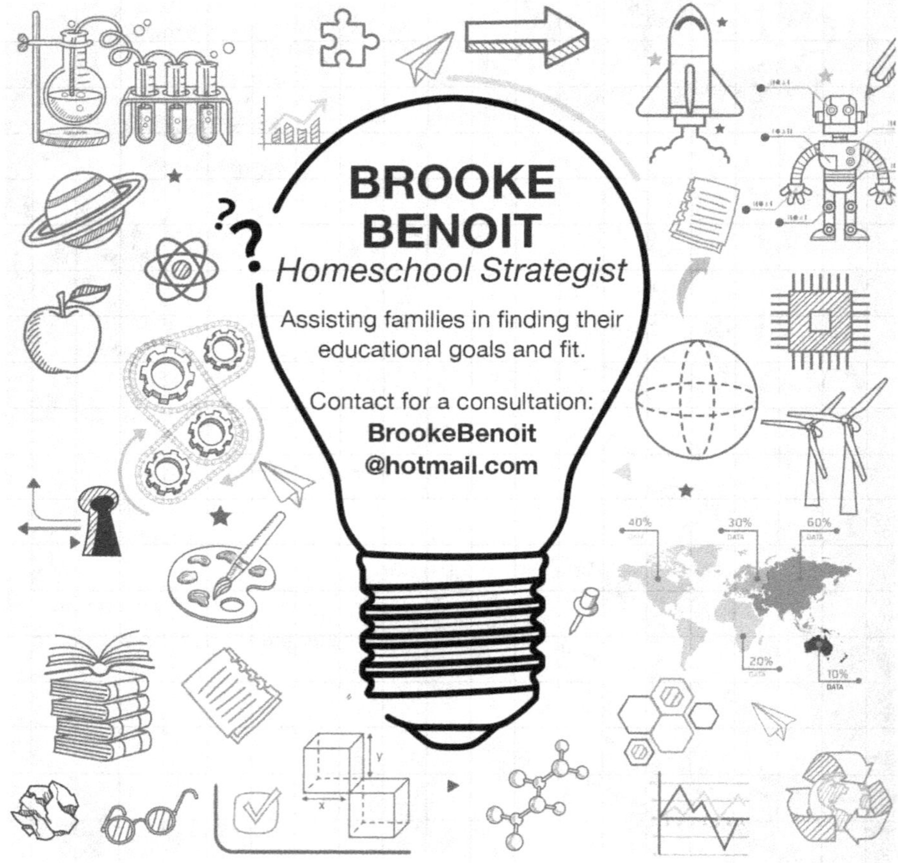
BROOKE
BENOIT
Homeschool Strategist
Assisting families in finding their
educational goals and fit.
Contact for a consultation:
BrookeBenoit
@hotmail.com
40%
30%
60%
20%
10%

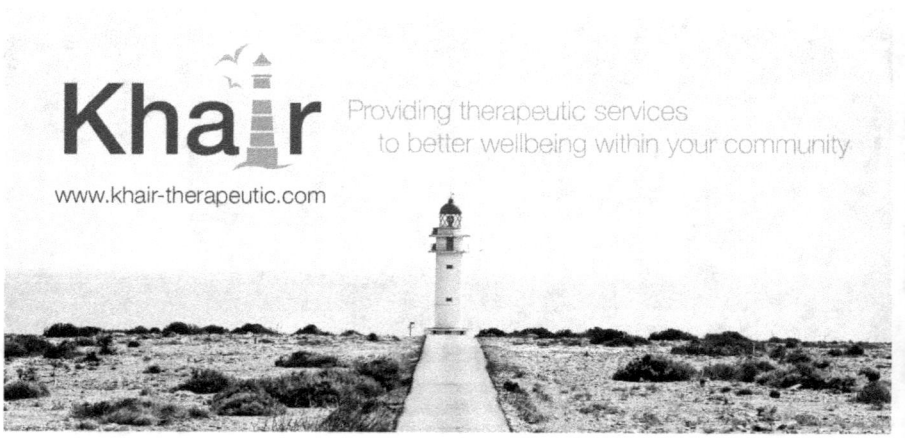

Khair
Providing therapeutic services
to better wellbeing within your community
www.khair-therapeutic.com

Chapter 3

SOCIALIZING, SUPPORT AND SELF-CARE

Yes, Socialization Can Be A Problem

By Jamila Alqarnain

The subject of socialization frequently pops up in the homeschool community. It seems we are always on the defense, trying to convince someone that homeschooled children have just as much opportunities to socialize with other kids as they would if they went to public school. We come up against the "What about socialization?" question not just from the anti-homeschool club, but also from worried parents who are considering the homeschool route. It's natural that we have become defensive about it. Having the same question asked over and over again can do that to a person. However, I feel like as homeschoolers, we are so sensitive about this subject that we spend most of our time defending ourselves and not addressing the fact that this can be an issue for some families.

Of course homeschooling does not mean a child has to be doomed to a life of solitude. We know that there are plenty of social butterflies having all sorts of awesome adventures in homeschooling. The issue is that not everyone is having a wonderful time of it. Not everyone's experience is the same. I think that the point should be made to parents considering homeschooling that it is really important to make sure kids have ample opportunity to get out of the house and be around their peers. Most of us simply do not realize that some families are having this problem. This is why I chose to address this unpopular and preferably ignored issue: to build awareness.

When I was working on my book *The Muslim Family Guide to Successful Homeschooling*, I interviewed adults who had been homeschooled when they were young children. Some complained about not getting out enough to be with other children. They felt that because of this they did not have valuable social skills. They were lonely, and unhappy with their homeschooling experience. I don't believe that their parents were lazy or unwilling to find outlets for the children. Parents may not know what to do with their children and there may not be a lot of other homeschoolers in the area.

One sister said she lived in a small town and there simply wasn't that much to do there. We all know that there are some Muslim women who, for whatever reason, just don't get out a lot. So when they start homeschooling they stay in their usual routine of being homebodies. These sisters need to hear about the importance of taking their kids on playdates, enrolling them in classes, joining co-ops, finding sport outlets, etc. There are questions that they should ask themselves before starting their journey: Are there any other families homeschooling in my area? What classes are offered in my area? If there just aren't a lot of opportunities for socialization locally, is relocating an option? Can we drive a little further out to meet up with other homeschooling families? What about our masjid? Is there a youth group or other opportunities for my child to socialize with other Muslim kids?

If parents come together and really give these things some thought, they will likely make a way to find plenty of opportunities for their kids to meet up with other kids. This may be more difficult for some than it is for others but it is still possible. We just have to make sure that we leave no stone unturned and take advantage of all the resources available to us.

The ultimate goal is make sure that our children have the best homeschool experience that we can provide. It is on us to ensure that their needs are being met and they are growing, not just academically, but spiritually and characteristically. In order to do that sometimes it takes strategic planning, especially when it's not clear where the tools we need to meet our children's needs are going to come from. Do some sleuthing around in your community. More than likely the answers are there. If we make lots of dua while looking for solutions Allah will make a way. He always does.

Jamila Alqarnain, a native of Buffalo, New York and a 2nd generation Muslim, was an active child whose hobbies included sewing, arts and crafts, reading, drawing and writing stories. Sewing was her favorite. Majoring in Fashion Clothing & Textiles at Buffalo Vocational Technical Center, her goal was to become a seamstress and fashion designer. However, as time passed, Jamila rediscovered her love of writing. She teamed up with her sister and co-founded Noon Publications. In 2005, she published her first book, The Muslim Family Guide to Successful Homeschooling. *Jamila has been a homeschooling mom since 2000. She is also a wife, blogger and entrepreneur.*

Finding The Right Pillars Of Support

By Angeliqua Rahhali

All new journeys must begin with a leap. Taking that leap may be the scariest or most exciting moment that you ever face. We hear of homeschooling and start to wonder what this might do for our families. You research until your mind can't take it anymore and then you research some more. This is a path that all of us homeschooling families have been down.

One question leads to five more questions that give you answers that then just create more questions, when all you were searching for was reassurance and solutions! While seeking advice from friends and family you will find everyone has an opinion about what you should or shouldn't be doing to raise your children. These opinions may be the hardest part of this journey to overcome. As you continue in your search you will find so many different schools of thought about homeschooling styles that it can be overwhelming. There will be information on almost every aspect of education from birth through the university years and beyond. One important aspect of being successful at any stage of your life will be having the right support system to guide and help you.

Just like in our spiritual journeys when we turn to those that came before us to help understand what we need for the path in front of us, the same goes for seeking guidance from others in educating our children.

There will be plenty of dark days on your homeschooling journey. At times you may feel like your kids have not learned anything that day or ever, but they are and they will. Part of the process of being a homeschooling family is understanding the need for non-structured learning and the benefits it can have in your routine and mental health. Some days will leave you exhausted and all efforts to study seem pointless. It is in those moments that having a great support system is vital. Having friends and family who you can turn to that understand your struggle will help you continue.

Aside from the emotional relief your support network can bring, practical support can lead to better mental health and an overall better functioning system within the family. Consider people who can help give you a little break while you regroup and recharge your own batteries. This may not be another family member, you may need a childcare provider. Support also comes in the form of outsourcing the actual teaching. Attempting to teach all subjects and to be an expert in all areas is not even required of school teachers, yet homeschoolers often think they need to do just that. Most teachers focus on one subject and students pass around from class to class. This method can be applied within the home learning system. You create the learning environment you want that works best for your family.

Every child will have different goals and ambitions, different learning styles and needs. Learning what helps your children to best succeed within their education will take time to develop. They do not come out of the womb knowing what they want or what their options are. Building great support systems includes finding other resources to turn to for ideas, motivation, and assistance.

Within my family I have found that our learning styles change with each year as our children grow and redefine what their views are of the world around them. With their needs changing as they age, their socialization needs and educational needs change as well. Finding balance within our home and our community has been the biggest obstacle to achieve but has led to the most memorable moments. One source that has been of great use has been to look at other adults around us and see how they have learned and taught themselves hobbies and activities that they were never introduced to in school. What things did they strive to learn outside of the educational system because there was just not enough time or any opportunity? As adults we are always learning new things to better our lives. We are not relying on specific teachers with grades and tests to dictate if we have learned something useful. We learn to adapt as we grow, as we mature through life and make mistakes. This is what learning is all about. Have faith that we can guide our children and show them how to love learning for themselves.

Throughout the years we have had the opportunity to move several times and have had the chance to add more friends to our inner support circle. Getting to know new neighbors is always a challenge and source of stress within itself, especially if they do not understand your religious beliefs let alone understand your views on education. It is natural to want to defend yourself and your way of thinking when expressing your reasons for homeschooling to new friends. You will find more people to be understanding and supportive of your choices as they see you succeed in your work. True friends and supporters will want to share in your happiness because they will know that what you want for yourself you want for others as well.

When children are young, before school age, parents do their best to find ways to let them interact with other children, such as looking for safe parks, scheduling play dates among friends and attending family gatherings filled with relatives of all ages. This is the beginning of forming a foundation full of people you feel comfortable turning to when you have parenting questions and needs. During this period, you make sure that everything you are doing for your child is in their best interest and will give them the greatest chances for success in the future. You will seek advice from other parents that can empathize with you and confirm that your stresses are not unique to your situation. Understanding what other people have gone through will help clear up some of your confusions and fears of child-rearing during the early stages of learning. Why would you not want the same support from your friends and family when it comes to educating your child?

You will find this is also the time others outside of your inner circle will readily voice their opinions on how you choose to educate your child. As your child becomes school-aged and the worries of growth milestones are no longer the key focus, most people turn their focus to educational milestones. They will have input on how and what you should be teaching your child and how your child will compare to theirs. One thing to keep in mind is that doing everything yourself can be fine in the beginning but can quickly lead to burnout. Having a support network of family and friends who understand your struggles will help to alleviate the stress that can be brought on during those time periods. Having support from others who agree with your homeschooling choices will help buffer this inevitable negativity brought on by those not comfortable with homeschooling.

When embarking on something new and unknown, like homeschooling, we assume that our spouses will support us one hundred percent and our families will have our backs no matter that our choices are far beyond the norm. There will be many heated discussions and debates, many moments of doubt and you may feel you need to validate your decision to home-school even within your immediate family. We easily forget in our excitement that this is new and unknown to many around us who are used to education coming in the form of institutional (public or private) schools. They are following the paradigm that education only fits one particular path, which will lead to college then a career and ultimately a successful life.

It is important to have patience with those around you and even yourself while you try to define what schooling means to you. In the beginning you will feel the need to always have to show and tell to prove your child's successes. Having a strong support system will be vital at this time. During this early stage you will forge bonds with people and exchange ideas. You will find yourself excited to wake up and want to play with goop and gunk. You will be proud of those burnt baked creations your child makes in an attempt to show their independence. The messes you come across will be less of a mess and more of an "artistic outlet". Your excitement will build their confidence in their exploratory learning and open doors to the future that they may not have been thinking about. For example, a child playing in the kitchen may not have thought they could go on to study culinary arts and be successful at it, or a child sewing their own doll clothes may go on to be a designer- and not just of clothes. You will begin to mentally connect these activities to more formal fields, such as Home Economics and find math activities in the most mundane of chores. Those tiny moments we take for granted will be the highlights of the week. During these times you need people that understand and can relate to your roller coaster of emotions and frustrations. Some days will seem like an endless uphill battle, but if you stop and think about it, anyone who has their kids home during an extended school break faces the same issues. The difference is you face these battles daily and won't be able to have a once or twice a year rant about it and move on. You need continual support.

Having your spouse on board and your family to turn to will be very important. If they are not understanding or respectful of your choices it will be much harder, but Allah (SWT) has put into us the urge to homeschool for a reason. We will never be given anything we cannot handle and if this is your battle, know that it is yours for a reason. Having other Muslim homeschooling families that are facing similar struggles will be a great place to turn to for support. If there is not an Islamic homeschooling community in your area, then don't be afraid to reach out and find other homeschooling families that you might be able to meet up with and pick their brains. Many cities now have meetup groups and co-ops that get together for activities and field trips. Insha Allah, there will be someone out there who will be your cup of tea and you can turn to for advice and guidance. You may have to work with non-Muslim groups and find other support networks online. With social media exploding into all aspects of life right now, there are just as many great support groups as there are areas of learning.

There will be times when everyone is in school and the playgrounds are empty and the parks are only filled with children not of school age. It can seem lonely for your child and for yourself as well. Not all that we learn comes from a book, learning is part of who we are and the way we live and interact with those around us. Sometimes we will long to be with and organically learn from others. When Islamic holidays come around that may fall outside of the regular scheduled holiday time, you don't have to worry about explaining to anyone why you are taking time out of your schedule to celebrate. Every gathering becomes an opportunity to learn stories from elders, and create new memories for generations to come. We are able to take more time to enjoy these special moments as life whizzes by.

When I think of what support means to me I look back to stories I was taught growing up that imparted lessons of why we need to stick together. One concept that stood out all these years later was that if you had a strand of fiber and pulled hard enough from both ends that eventually you would break it, but if you put a bunch of fibers together and twisted them into a rope and then tried to pull that, it would take tremendous strength to break it. This is what having a good support system does. It gives you strength in the weakest of times.

Allah (SWT) put us on this path for a reason. We will stumble and fall, but we will also succeed inshaAllah. We have to try, try, and try again until we find what works for us, and in doing so trust that the gaps will get filled in over time. Everyone has a destiny unfolding for them in their own time. When you give your child access to the untapped corners of their mind and give them the right key to open the doors of knowledge, you will see their eyes light up and that moment is so precious. In those moments you will feel blessed to be chosen for this path. It is your journey, but you will find others traversing it, and they can be the support that will help you to leap forward and not let others hold you back from succeeding.

Angeliqua Rahhali is an artist, home-educator, counselor, cultural anthropologist, writer and explorer. She loves learning and can often be found researching everything, from how things are made and where they come from, to the next destination she wants to learn about and culture to embrace. She loves reading, playing brain games and experimenting with fusions of flavors in her kitchen.

12 Steps To Practicing Vital Self-Care

By Khalida Haque

"You cannot pour from an empty cup." - Anonymous

What is self-care?
Self-care is seen as a habit that enables well-being. According to the National Health Service it means: "Looking after yourself in a healthy way, whether it's brushing your teeth, taking medicine when you have a cold, or doing some exercise". It is done intentionally and purposefully. And it is of holistic benefit.

Self-care is also a divine responsibility. Our bodies and selves, just as everything else, that Allah (SWT) has bestowed upon us, are an amanah (a trust) upon us. When I think of self-care, I remember the following two ahadith:

The Prophet (SAW) once asked a companion: "(Is it true) that you fast all day and stand in prayer all night?" The companion replied that the report was indeed true. The Prophet then said: "Do not do that! Observe the fast sometimes and also leave (it) at other times. Stand up for prayer at night and also sleep at night. Your body has a right over you, your eyes have a right over you and your wife has a right over you." *(Bukhari)*

In the second hadith, Hanzalah (RA) reported, "Abu Bakr met me and asked: How are you O Hanzalah? I replied, "Hanzalah is guilty of hypocrisy!" He said, "Free is Allah and far removed from all defects! What are you saying?" I said, "When we are with Allah's Messenger (SAW) and he reminds us of the Fire and Paradise it is as if we were seeing it with our own eyes. Then when we depart from Allah's Messenger (SAW) and attend our wives, our children and our business, then much of this slips from our mind." Abu Bakr said, "By Allah we also experience the same."

I went with Abu Bakr until we entered upon Allah's Messenger (SAW). I said, "Hanzalah is guilty of hypocrisy O Messenger of Allah (SAW)." Allah's Messenger (SAW) said, "And how is that?" I said, "When we are with you, you remind us of the Fire and of Paradise and it is as if we are seeing it with our own eyes. Then when we depart from you and attend our wives, our children and our business then much of this slips from our minds." And Allah's Messenger (SAW) said, "By Him in whose hand is my soul if you remained continually as you are when you are with me and in remembering (Allah) then the angels would shake hands with you upon your beds and upon your roads. But O Hanzalah, (there is) a time for this and a time for that, (there is) a time for this and a time for that, (there is) a time for this and a time for that." *(Muslim)*

It is difficult to be strong when we are spent and empty. And as we know through hadith, the strong believer is better and more beloved to Allah than the weak believer *(Muslim)*. This strength refers to an internal strength and relates to *imaan* (faith) which becomes eroded if there is no self love and compassion. Everyone has an internal voice and it is often negative. It is generally an internalisation of a critical parent. This voice, this harsh inner critic that many, if not all, of us possess is not as influential if we take care of ourselves. It loses power if we practice self-care, though it may try to sabotage us when we do. This voice does not believe we are deserving of care, love, affection or indeed anything positive.

I don't think it is possible to express just how important looking after ourselves is.

Selfishness

"Taking care of yourself is the best selfish thing you can do" -*Unknown*

Self-care is often confused with selfishness and when someone does something for themselves they can often feel guilty. There is a gulf of difference between doing something for self absorbed, narcissistic personal gain and doing something that allows us to recharge, replenish and feel human once more. When we are being selfish we are showing a lack of consideration for others and our primary concern is our own profit and/or pleasure. Genuine self-care is not selfish. True self-care is nurturing, honouring, caring for, and loving ourselves - both for our own benefit and for those around us.

Homeschooling and self-care

"Taking good care of you means that the people in your life will get the best of you rather than what's left of you." -*Carl Bryan, Tennis Coach*

If we reflect upon the above ahadith, we recognise that we have to divide and devise our time wisely and that a fair portion needs to be given to each aspect of our lives, selves and commitments. As mothers we are often the worst at self-care because, let's face it, we basically place ourselves at the bottom of the list; right there at the bottom of the heap, below the ironing and taking out the rubbish. And playing the martyr then comes so easily to many of us: "Look at poor me who is doing everything for everyone". We often tell ourselves that self-care is something we should do when we get everything else done. When we have some time for it. However it is important that we recognize that we have to make time for it. It cannot be an add-on or afterthought.

Sometimes we may be motivated to take care of ourselves out of guilt or fear: I really should eat better. I really ought to exercise more. I'm not taking very good care of myself and if I continue this way I'm going to get sick, gain weight or something terrible is going to happen to me. And as these negative, critical thoughts roll around in our heads they often become the impetus or motivation for us to "take care of ourselves." However, it is better if we choose to take care of ourselves rather than feel forced into it.

Experience, theory and practice all say that a happy mum makes for happy children. Therefore, it is really important for us to take care of ourselves if we are not only mothers, but also homeschoolers. Teachers who work in schools are drained by the end of the day. So what does that say for mothers who homeschool? They don't get time away from the children and the classroom, particularly if there are no boundaries between mum time, learning time, play time, etc. And these mums don't self-care and put themselves in the 'I'll get to it when I have time' list. There is a very interesting phenomenon, probably something to do with quantum physics ... or more likely *barakah* (blessings), but when we earnestly spend out of our time (be it on ourselves or others) then our time seems to expand. We may have little of it but it can be rich and full. However, it is not just the quality of our time that can grow. The way we are stands to also benefit.

Self-care is not only essential to our personal well-being but it is fundamental for our relationships with others, particularly those closest to us. And as expressed earlier, it enriches us and what we are able to give to others. We cannot give anything if we are drained and working from reserves. Contemplate how you are with your children when you haven't slept the night before and are plain exhausted. How the slightest thing can tip you into the abyss of negative parenting. Would that happen (so often) if we recognised that we needed to take care of ourselves, just for a few minutes? Self-care can empower us to be more generous and available with those around us in an authentic, true to ourselves manner, whilst modelling to them how we want to be treated.

Taking care of ourselves requires willingness, commitment, and courage. Given the nature of our often busy, bustling lives it's not always logistically or emotionally possible for us to even make, let alone keep, our self-care promises. Therefore it is imperative for us to recognise that it is not about doing it perfectly or right, or even about following a detailed plan to the very letter. It is more about remembering ourselves and that we deserve to take care of ourselves. And that when we do, it not only nourishes and replenishes us but also allows us to be available for those important things and people in our lives. As mothers and homeschoolers those things and people are our children and their education.

How to self-care

"Sometimes the most important thing in a whole day is the rest we take between two deep breaths." - *Etty Hillesum*

Truly, taking care of ourselves can be as simple as that. When we focus on ensuring our 'rest' we tend to have the strength for all the other stuff in our lives. Below is a list of suggested twelve steps to self-care that are readily available on the internet. I've added a few of my own thoughts and explanations.

1. If it feels wrong, don't do it

This first step requires us to get to know ourselves and to trust our instincts. If it feels wrong, at the very least entertain the feeling and give yourself the time to think about it. What's the rush anyway? You'll miss out?

'Umar Ibn Al-Khattab is reported to have said: "No amount of guilt can change the past, and no amount of worrying can change the future. Go easy on yourself, for the outcome of all affairs is determined by Allah's decree. If something is meant to go elsewhere, it will never come your way, but if it is yours by destiny, from it you cannot flee."

2. Say exactly what you mean

Too often we don't actually say what we mean. More likely we say what we think others want to hear. If we don't say what we mean how are others to understand our needs? And who can we then blame when they then do things against our wishes? Be clear.

3. Don't be a people pleaser
The things we do and say are usually for the pleasure of others. We like to see others happy. But does it have to be at the expense of ourselves? When we are people pleasing we are putting ourselves at the bottom of the list.

4. Trust your instincts
Our instincts are there for a reason. And the only book we truly need to be able to read is ourselves. It will ultimately tell us so much about others. Too often we say "I wish I'd followed my gut" about dealing with others and making choices.

5. Never speak badly about yourself
We all make mistakes but to speak badly of yourself means that you are not recognising the things about yourself for which to be grateful. Also why would you want to speak badly of yourself? Sometimes we do it to illicit sympathy from others and it can be manipulative. And being manipulated causes others to feel bad about themselves. Consider your feelings when you've heard someone talk about themselves negatively.

6. Never give up on your dreams
Dreams provide us with hope. Aspirations give us something to work towards. Having a focus and a goal can pull you back up when you've been knocked down.

7. Don't be afraid to say no
If you don't want to do something or you can't, just say no. Saying no can be really hard for those of us who are people pleasers and do not like the idea of letting someone down. However, you will without a doubt be letting yourself and others down if you are doing things you don't want to or if you overstretch yourself.

8. Don't be afraid to say yes
Particularly to yourself. If you want something and can afford it carefully consider why not say yes?

9. Be kind to yourself
If you cannot be kind to yourself then what sort of kindness are you truly showing others? Kindness to others without kindness to ourselves is often borne out of guilt, self-blame and people pleasing. Kindness to ourselves shows us the true way to be kind to others. But be kind to yourself anyway, you've probably had a hard day! Also see the earlier reported saying of 'Umar Ibn Al-Khattab.

10. Let go of what you can't control
In the psychotherapy world we talk about spheres of control. There is the sphere of things within our control and a sphere that is outside. There is also an overlap area which is referred to as an area of influence. We may be able to influence but we cannot control. The idea is that we take care of everything within our sphere of control and leave to others their spheres. And sometimes all that is in our ability is to let go because we can choose to do that.

11. Stay away from drama and negativity
Drama and negativity is draining. It will sap you and bleed you dry. So do your best to sidestep it and walk away.

12. LOVE
Love yourself. Love others. Just love. Love makes everything easier.

And now four things to focus on in terms of self-care:

How we treat ourselves
We need to treat ourselves the way we'd treat someone we love. Think about how you speak to yourself. Would you talk that way to anyone you cared about? Self-blame and negativity is unproductive and when we recognise this it can be very powerful. If we continue with the self harshness it actually moves us away from the things we want to achieve. Consider someone of authority, say a teacher, constantly on your case and demeaning you: how motivated would you be? Now think about a teacher who encouraged, supported and nurtured you, how would you be then? Our minds cannot distinguish between thought and external event. So we hear negative self-talk and experience it similarly. Therefore, it is important that we make sure that our self-talk is loving, supportive, nurturing, and forgiving. It will take some time for us to believe and it will be like hearing a story we know well being told completely differently – confusing and possibly distressing. However, in time we can unlearn and re-train our thought processes to become healthy and helpful. Treat yourself with the utmost respect, you deserve it!

Health and feeling well
Physical and emotional wellbeing are intrinsically linked. We obsess far too much about our external appearances and achieving the perfect body. Instead we ought to focus on what being healthy gives us and how it makes us feel, then we are more likely to feel motivated and stay on track as well as find a deeper sense of gratification. We also start to become intolerant of how unhealthy choices cause us to feel. This leads to us being able to reframe the way we look at healthy options. Self-care requires us to nourish and feed ourselves physically and emotionally. And if we eat well and exercise we are likely to feel our best and thus banish any concerns of ill health. Exercise, of any form, is known to release endorphins (the happy hormone), fight anxiety, as well as leave us feeling good. Moments of stillness and quiet, no matter how brief, enable us to find inner calm and peace. If you are physically and emotionally well you can be more available for others and you can partake in more activities.

Stay positive and be grateful
Don't waste time and emotion looking at others and wishing you had what they have. If you need visual inspiration for a physical change then find photos of you at your best or perhaps hang up a dress you would like to get back into. If there's a holiday you want to take then have a picture of it as your wallpaper on your laptop. If you want your children to all go to university create a picture of them doing that (in your minds). Learn to release the negativity and focus on all the good you have and on all that you've achieved. Make a daily list of your accomplishments and what you are grateful for. By doing this it will motivate us to do more and help us when we start to feel frustrated and ready to give up. Nothing is too small to be grateful for especially if it is moving you in the right direction.

Love yourself
We need to learn to love ourselves. To do this we need to acknowledge our efforts and achievements and see perfection in our 'imperfections'. We need to find the beauty within ourselves. To love ourselves we need to catch our negative thoughts and release them, not hold on to them. It may seem ironic but when we focus on caring and loving ourselves the external transformation, (we've perhaps been craving), is more likely to occur. When we treat ourselves with the care and respect we deserve the routines needed for a physical transformation to take place seem to naturally develop. Similarly you will be able to be more available for your loved ones or think more creatively in terms of the education of your child(ren). Because you are grateful for what you have, you will make choices that benefit you and your family.

We are fortunate as Muslims that we have built-in time to regroup, recoup and recharge in the form of our daily prayers. I know that as mothers, particularly with little ones, praying in peace is a luxury but if we can enable ourselves to have even a moment of *kushoo* (calmness, serenity) then it can do wonders for our day and our general presence.

"Your time is limited, so don't waste it living someone else's life. Don't be trapped by dogma - which is living with the results of other people's thinking. Don't let the noise of others' opinions drown out your own inner voice. And most importantly, have the courage to follow your heart and intuition. They somehow already know what you truly want to become. Everything else is secondary."
- *Steve Jobs*

Islamically, we know that we need to submit to the will of Allah (SWT) but do we recognize that that will has given us the permission to be who we are? And so we need to also submit to who we are. Because it is all contained within us, we have to have those moments of self-care that allow for self-reflection and contemplation to unravel ourselves. When we know ourselves better we are better placed to help our children discover who they are.

Khalida Haque is a qualified and experienced counselling psychotherapist who has a private practice, is a clinical supervisor, group facilitator, freelance writer and counselling services manager as well as founder and managing director of Khair.

Chapter 4
FURTHER OUTSIDE THE BOX

Single-Parent Homeschooling

By Samar Asamoah

It's not about the pros and cons, it's about what suits us.

For me, homeschooling is about taking responsibility for my children's education. I'm not saying that parents who choose to send their children to school are irresponsible. What I'm saying is I'm not afraid to take it all on myself. Recently a family relative suggested (or actually they ordered me to!) that I should send my children to school. They said that they are scared that my children won't be able to go to university or study sciences if they are homeschooled. I could tell that they had absolutely no knowledge whatsoever about the many opportunities that homeschooled children have compared to those in school. When I started to explain the process and to send them links showing cases of home educated children going to uni as early as the age of twelve, it still didn't seem to reassure them. Is it perhaps because I'm a single parent?

I started homeschooling about five years ago. My daughter was seven at the time and both she and my son, then age three, had just come back from a long family holiday of about five months. I felt that I needed to get my daughter back into school because that's normally just what you do. My son quickly got a place in nursery but I was told I would have to wait a few weeks before I found out if my daughter had been accepted into a school. I decided that in the meantime we would work at home together so she wouldn't fall behind. I bought some books and found some online resources. My daughter and I worked together doing maths, English, and science. I found it quite easy, it was like helping with homework after school. Since she was only seven, it was simple enough stuff. When we did get the acceptance letter from the school my daughter looked at me and said: "Mama I don't wanna go back to school, I want to be homeschooled." Remarkably, I simply responded: "OK then".

It wasn't a difficult decision for me to take as I was unemployed at the time, so having the time wasn't an issue. Not only that, but I was more than happy to continue as we were because really I had wanted to homeschool my children even before I had them. When I gave birth to my daughter I was at university and it was just easier to put my daughter into nursery and school than follow my preference. As for my son, I kept him in school; he finished nursery and went on to reception. He was doing very well and seemed to enjoy it for the most part - he had friends, an excellent school report and exceptional social skills for a child his age. However after seeing all the fun things that his sister was doing at home and hearing about our homeschooling trips, he started asking if he could be homeschooled too.

I didn't want to take him out of school before the year was over so I told him to wait till it was over. I actually thought that he would change his mind but he never did. To be honest I have been both surprised and pleased with my children in this respect: they rarely change their minds about what they want to do and are quite driven once they decide something. This has been a very useful trait with regards to their home education. There is a three-year gap between them and my daughter being the elder is very good at tutoring her brother as well as self-study. One of the best ways to reinforce your own learning is to teach others. Educators know this, but schools seldom have the time or resources to engage in peer-tutoring activities. I do spend one-on-one time with each of them but my daughter does a lot more self-study on her own inclination. She is currently learning Japanese by herself. My son also enjoys learning different languages and diverse subjects such as graphic design, sciences, and arts.

I actually feel that as a single parent I can spend more time with my children because I homeschool them. I no longer have the burden of the morning or afternoon school rush. I'm not confined by the school holidays as to when I can travel with my kids or not. Education is a way of life for us, it is notjust confined to a particular building, time or place. I can juggle my self-employment with homeschooling pretty easily. No doubt it can be hard sometimes but that's probably more because I take on other activities not related to my home life because I'm quite driven as an individual. These are usually short term projects though and I think as a parent it's good to show your children that you are also trying to improve yourself.

I'm sure that two-parent families also have their struggles as well as their strengths. I think the most important thing as a family is working together as a team. Once you have good teamwork in place anything is possible.

Samar Asamoah is an African Caribbean revert and self-employed single mum raising multicultural kids in the north of England. Her artwork and Eid cards for Syria are available at etsy.com/shop/Yezarck.

At Last, Homeschooling My Child With Dyslexia

By Ann Stock Ghazy

It was in Cairo that I had my first glimpse of the inner workings of the mysterious homeschooling underworld and the mothers who dwell within them. They are an unusual bunch, which is good because I have always liked unusual people. I resisted the common sense reasoning of these moms and the evidence of success they provided me for many years because... it was just... well... you know... not my cup of tea. "But I don't wanna..." came out of my mouth every time I was approached about one of their alternatives to traditional schooling, especially that zany idea of unschooling. It wasn't until I had been pushed into a corner that I even considered homeschooling for my children. It would be more accurate to say that I held onto the door frame as I was dragged kicking and screaming into the homeschooling underworld.

The biggest problem with homeschooling, I thought, was giving up my freedom. There is something normal and comforting about saying good-bye to your children in the morning and having the whole day to do what you need to do, like taking those Qur'an classes you have always wanted to take, getting back to your career, perhaps picking up the house and having it stay that way for longer than five minutes, or meeting friends for coffee. I had a lot of self doubts too. I couldn't visualize myself setting up a classroom and running a school from my house. How many hours would that take? Also, class preparations and organizing a syllabus seemed overwhelming. What if I didn't know how to teach the math lesson? Who would teach him Arabic and Quran? Maybe I wouldn't be patient and I would do more harm than good. Would I be consistent or would I get lazy over time? What if I hated it and my child missed out on a year of his education? Moreover, Middle Eastern countries do not recognize homeschooling, which meant that my child attending a university in Egypt would not be an option. The risks seemed too big. No, I was pretty certain homeschooling wasn't for me, but no one knows what tomorrow will bring.

My son, who is the youngest of my seven children, gave me a hard time from day one when it came to his school work. Throughout early elementary his performance was dismal. He was having difficulty reading, writing and generally trying to keep up with his classmates. His teachers and I felt that he would eventually catch on if only he would work a little harder. However, I knew deep inside something was wrong. I fought these natural feelings because I am a big worrywort when it comes to my children and I kept reminding myself not to overreact, yet again. After all, when speaking to him he seemed just fine. He was bright, curious and always off having adventures on our farm. He was normal in every other way. Surely he was just a playful boy.

When my husband was hired in Jeddah, Saudi Arabia, we needed to transfer our children to new schools. It was a teacher, in charge of entrance exams, who first noticed my son's problem for what it was. After years of struggling to get him to read and write properly, after having his eyesight checked and his hearing tested, the obvious reason lay so clearly before me. He wasn't lazy about work and just playful. It wasn't that he didn't try hard enough. His brain was wired differently. After we had him tested it was confirmed, he had dyslexia and dysgraphia.

I felt guilty that I had not identified it myself, but I felt relieved that there were people out there who are willing to explain what the problem is and how to help me help him. Dyslexia is often misunderstood. It is not a lag in the ability to understand. Dyslexics are often very bright. It is a chronic condition. It is the way in which the brain is wired, and it has to be dealt with in a systematic way to enable the person to have a functioning reading level. After all, reading is a learned skill not a natural ability like speaking. There are many ways to teach someone how to read but schools don't have time to cater and are slow to change.

Phonology, the smallest unit of sound like 'a' as in "apple" for example, is exactly the source of the problem for a dyslexic. They are not able to break a word apart and see its individual sounds. So if they see "cat" they do not see it as c-a-t. They see it as a solid picture "cat". Kind of like seeing the building but not realizing it is made of individual bricks. In particular, they have trouble distinguishing the different vowel sounds. To compensate, they often look at the first letter and retrieve from their mind any word starting with that letter. According to Sally Shaywitz, MD, who works with dyslexia at Yale University, "70 to 80 percent of American children learn how to transform printed symbols into phonetic decode without much difficulty. For the rest of the students it remains a mystery." Those 20 to 30 percent are the people with dyslexia, and that was my son.

After extensive research, it has been discovered how to accommodate the dyslexic brain. There is a system and a process they have developed enabling people with dyslexia to learn the steps needed for reading, but it needs early intervention and lots of repetition until the word is properly stored in the brain. This manual method works but it time-intensive. This presented a problem for my son and me.

At first I tried to work with him in the evenings after he came home from school, but he was often too tired to cooperate with me. As a result, he kept falling further and further behind. The school systems in the Middle East generally do not recognize learning differences like dyslexia. It became self evident that homeschooling was his best chance to regain his confidence and have a real education. After years of labor and out of pure necessity, a new homeschooling mom was born into this world.

Homeschooling moms are great at networking, helping each other in various ways, and even encouraging being good Muslims. Their unique bonds of sisterhood make their relationships even tighter. This was a huge help and a great gift to me because once I knew homeschooling was the option I had to take, then I needed to see what exact direction I wanted to go. I needed expert advice and there is plenty of that to be had from most homeschooling moms who are more than happy to give advice to anyone who will listen. Through this process of asking lots of questions from everyone I knew of, I met a sister who also was a homeschooling adviser/coach. We discussed the options that were available. Did I want to unschool? What about a traditional homeschooling program like Calvert or others like it? Or should I use one of the online home schools in which the assignments were arranged by the school and graded by a teacher on the other end of cyberspace? Or should I use an eclectic approach, which is selecting and using what I considered the best elements of all systems? There was a lot to consider, so armed with an assortment of books and a head full of advice, I began to sift through things until I came up with what worked best for us.

Living abroad presents itself with a unique set of problems which my new friend and homeschooling adviser had already plowed through. She filled me in on her research and the solutions to the unique problems of sisters homeschooling abroad. Our problems are multifaceted including: a lack of public lending libraries, unreliable postal service, high import tax on equipment and books (I experienced this in Egypt, but not in the Kingdom of Saudi Arabia), lengthy screening of imported books which often leads to their confiscation for unknown reasons and with no apologies either.

An online homeschooling program was the best solution for us. Our family lives in Jeddah, Saudi Arabia during the academic year and back in Cairo for the summers. It was a big benefit to not have actual textbooks taking up space and weight in the luggage. I also didn't want to come up with my own syllabus because I too am a student and felt I wouldn't have time to do a good job. The online school had a syllabus and would grade assignments and give feedback from within one to three days. This allowed me to focus on my son's reading and writing. The best aspect of having his textbooks online is the ability to manipulate the page on the computer screen. We are able to enlarge the print and use readers for difficult passages which has given my son a little more independence. He also developed a little self-help system for confronting his dysgraphia (problem with spelling). After he writes a passage, he goes through and looks at the spell check suggestions and grammar corrections, then he opens the reader and listens to what he wrote to see if it is saying what he wanted it to say. When he has taken it through those three steps, he brings his work to me for a final check.

To make our homeschooling program more interesting, we often go off on tangents. For example we were studying rocks and one of the rocks mentioned was flint which can be used to start fires. Knowing that my son loved survival programs and equipment we began to explore more facts about flint rock and how to use it to make a fire when you are out in the wilderness without matches. This research and experimentation lasted a few days, giving my son a much needed boost, as schooling is not his favorite thing.

My fear of homeschooling was unwarranted. I thought I would lose eight hours of every day but in fact schools don't actually teach students for eight hours. We are able to finish most of my son's daily work in just two to three hours. He takes an additional hour to work on assignments and to submit his work. He actually studies more than he would if he were in school in less than half of the time. According to long-time homeschooler Reagan Ramm, "of the 7 hours spent locked away inside a public school building, approximately only 2 and a quarter of those hours are really spent being given instruction. Nearly 5 hours are wasted."

In the beginning I was afraid of not being able to pursue my studies. With my son in need of help with his reading, he is not always able to study when I am not home or when I am too busy. We killed two birds with one stone by solving this problem. I arranged for my son to attend a Qur'an memorizing school for the three hours while I am in class in the mornings. We come home together and begin his school work. Because we work at our own pace, if I have an exam or need time to do a heavy assignment, we can take a day off. The school provides video instruction for difficult concepts which means he doesn't always need me. If that doesn't work, there are so many resources which can be had at the touch of a key on Youtube. Although I am not always patient, as I feared, homeschooling has given me the opportunity to learn how to be more patient. I was worried that I wouldn't continue the commitment with my son but so far, a year and a half later, we are still on track.

I wanted to share our journey and what we have learned through tears, compromise, and adjustment. It isn't easy teaching a child with dyslexia and it isn't easy being one either. My son's experience in school was unpleasant at best. He still has a lot of confidence issues from the emotional abuse that he and other challenged children often face at schools by teachers and peers alike. We have had a lot of ups and downs but we have learned so much about each other and how to study, motivate and organize ourselves this past year. It hasn't always been easy and it still isn't, but it has always been worth it. My only regret is that I didn't homeschool all of my children using an eclectic approach.

Ann Lambert Stock lives back and forth between Cairo and Jeddah with her Egyptian husband. She is a freelance writer who regularly contributes to SISTERS magazine and is working on a four-part caliph series with Learning Roots to be released in the summer of 2016. You can follow her at Musings of a Muslimah umameerblog.wordpress.com

[i] Overcoming Dyslexia, Sally Shaywitz, M.D. (Codirector of the Yale Center for the Study of Learning and Attention, First Vintage Books Edition, January 2005

"Time Wasted In School: Outside of Class" https://coastalconservatory.com/2015/09/24/time-wasted-in-school-outside-of-class/

Why I Still Homeschool In A Muslim Country

By Brooke Benoit

The call of the *athan*, plentiful halal foods, people who know about Allah (SWT) similar to how you do, easier access to Islamic or Arabic resources for the entire family, and of course sending your kids to schools with Muslim teachers and peers are among the perks of repatriating or making hijrah to The Lands of The Muslims. Scratch out that last bit for me and the growing handful of families who choose to homeschool even over here.

For many Muslim families who homeschool in the West, they expect to discontinue doing so once they move abroad as if all the reasons they chose to homeschool in the first place will be left behind. It shouldn't come as much of a surprise that all the reasons are present in the 'East' too, where the Western model of education is mostly replicated and this is exactly why so many expats and locals are continuing or choosing to homeschool.

Growing Pains?
When freshly relocated expats complain about the conditions they find in the schools locally available to them, whether the curriculum, the general ethics or particulars of the staff, often more experienced expats will appease these complaints with something like, "You'll find a fit. You just have to keep looking." By 'fit' I think they may mean another sort of compromise, such as with more drive time or maybe that's just code for 'You'll get used to it' as so many seemed to do. For former homeschoolers like Charlene Gray, who homeschooled in Australia but initially enrolled her daughter in schools in Morocco, she knew that there was no reason to compromise her daughter's education when she found the school environments to be lacking in demonstrating Islamic principles as well as below her own standards of academics. Now Charlene's daughter is back to flourishing, as we know homeschoolers usually do.

Corporal punishment? No, Thanks
Another common thread of discussion I see among expats is about their kids being abused or bullied in school. This is something nearly every expat family I know of in my region has experienced. They have absolutely experienced it as far as other children bullying, throwing rocks at and fighting with each other, which I agree is a part of childhood that is unavoidable. I regularly deal with these kinds of problems outside of school hours, so would hate to think that my children were experiencing more while in school, but they would, and worse is that it happens at the hands of the adults who are supposed to educate them.

Just as discrimination is illegal in the states but still regularly happens, corporal punishment within schools is illegal in the region I live in but happens very regularly. Many parents deal with this by confronting their children's teachers, often more than once and sometimes resulting in physical altercations. One such fistfight with her child's (male!) principal is what led an expat friend of mine to return to homeschooling even though she obviously had thought she could quit once she made hijrah. This may sound like a worse-off scenario, but unfortunately it is common when the parents choose to confront their children's educators. Even if you are successful in your campaign and your child is no longer being abused by the teacher, they are still sitting among other students who are being emotionally and/or physically abused. While I want for your child what I want for my own, currently the best I can do with these circumstances is to home-educate.

What about socialization?

Daily incidents of bullying was just one paradigm shift motivator for unschooler and prolific writer Sadaf Farooqi who admits on her blog that sometimes her child (when younger) was even on the offensive side of bullying. While many non-homeschoolers cite concerns about lack of socialization as a reason not to homeschool, Sadaf, saw that her schooled child's socialization was being adversely affected as her pre-primary daughter "…had more problems than improvement in her social 'interactions' (fights and conflicts) with peers…" as socialization in institutionalized school settings has multiple problems. As Sadaf has explained in the comments of her blog, "I personally think it's debatable whether school improves social interaction. I think at the pre-primary and primary level, school actually curbs confidence, because such small kids rarely get to 'socialize' with each other freely only before first class, during break and in the short time after school before they are picked up. The rest of the time, any endeavor to 'socialize' innocently is strictly curbed by supervising teachers, and if continued, even results in that child being labelled as 'naughty' and 'disobedient'."

Sadaf discovered the concept of homeschooling through several teachers who, like many pioneers of the homeschooling movement in the US, chose to homeschool their own children instead of forcing them to sit through years of substandard and even abusive educational environments, or they became ardent advocates for others to homeschool. Sadaf has become a semi-reluctant key figure in the steadily growing homeschool community in her native Pakistan, be sure to check out her blog (and the next article in this issue!) for lots of insight both on general unschooling and specifically homeschooling in Pakistan.

It's a Muslim thing

Another homeschooling and writer friend, Maria Zain, began her homeschooling journey in Malaysia and now continues in the UK. Maria perfectly sums up many of my own reasons for home-educating, even in the Lands of the Muslims, "After 6 years of homeschooling, I've had time to put in much thought as to why I have chosen it, and I believe, first and foremost, it's because I believe that it falls upon the responsibility of parents to be the primary educators of their children, not the state's or the institution. I think parents have lost a lot of their parenting skills, due to pawning off their children to schools at too young an age, for too long a period of their waking time, that both parents and children have lost the true value of education, which encompasses so much more than textbook - classroom learning. Our religion puts so much honour in parents - children have to be THE BEST to their parents up until old age, but I would like to question many adults (including myself), have we done enough to deserve this type of honour and respect from our own offspring? A "parent" is not just a noun, it's also a verb, and adults need to honour this by being cohesively involved and understanding of their children's growth and development.

Secondly, another belief - Islam champions the great diversity of the ummah. In fact, the strength of the ummah lies in the diverse heritage of its people. While other religions struggle with supremacy of certain races and caste systems, Islam has zero tolerance for discrimination against race, nor against genders (men and women are spiritually equal), nor age, nor upbringing. The same should be taught for the diversity of talents, interests, specialisations (all within Shari'ah of course). Homeschooling provides the platform for children to develop at their own pace and pursue their interests without prejudice or judgement. When children are encouraged to do things that they love and are given the time and space to explore, they flourish a lot more as compared to learning under stress and timelines."

Ultimately my *Best Reason to Homeschool While Living in the Lands of the Muslims* is this: I like homeschooling. I enjoy encouraging my children's diverse interests and talents, I believe in my role to be their primary educator (along with my husband) and know that there is plenty of support available to us to do it, so I do.

Yes, of course homeschooling is exhausting and I have plenty of days in which I fantasize about the relief I may feel if I just put my kids in school. Ultimately this is one area of my life where I can delay gratification, insha Allah my relief will come later, but there is already plenty of joy and gratitude in the *right now*. Plus my kids say they "won't get on the yellow bus" so I'm stuck with it.

Brooke Benoit is running her own private Sudbury-like school with her seven children on the southern coast of Morocco. After this article was originally written for Brooke's neglected blog, Maria Zain passed away (inna lillahi wa inna 'ilayhi raji'un), her husband is still committed to homeschooling their now six children, insha Allah.

Unschooling In Pakistan: Like A Fish Out Of Water

By Sadaf Farooqi

What does it mean to be an unschooler, a niqab-wearer, and a Pakistani woman - all at the same time? Well, for starters, it gives rise to a feeling of being totally different from most of your peers; to be largely (and often) misunderstood by most; and to repeatedly be perceived as an unfathomable paradox. In short: I tend to feel like a fish out of water!

An introduction

I am a 37-year-old work-from-home author and freelance writer who began my writing career after marriage and motherhood, after I started staying at home with my two children who were born a little over two years apart: a daughter first, then a son. The roller-coaster journey of new motherhood was not easy, to say the least, but it was incredibly rewarding. However, in the beginning, I was rather overwhelmed. Every apparent 'cloud' has a hidden silver lining, does it not? Well, in my case, the challenging and rewarding journey of motherhood had more in store for my personal growth than I had imagined! As it turns out, the dilemma of not easily being able to go out somewhere on my own with my two children (both aged under three) in tow, without getting burned out and very stressed out, had a prominent silver lining: I started to turn to the Internet more and more while at home, to read in my spare time (particularly mommy blogs, where experienced mothers gave helpful practical tips about raising babies and toddlers), and eventually, to start my own writing endeavors: blogging and freelance article writing for different magazines.

My writing career aside, a few more years down the road, after I had put my firstborn in school - here in Pakistan, it is customary for the literati and educated families to admit their children into schools at ages as young as one or two years old - the challenges I had to face while searching for the most appropriate methodology for my child's education and upbringing led to my stumbling upon another, hitherto-undiscovered silver lining: the concept of homeschooling. And that is how the ball began to roll for me, for what I now refer to as my major 'twin' projects in life, which have become my primary occupations: writing and homeschooling.

Teething problems - a new start

At first, when I began to homeschool, I went mostly by trial and error, reading up about homeschooling online and adhering to the advice of experienced homeschoolers, instead of following my own maternal gut instincts. Like most nouveau home educating parents, I tried to replicate at home the traditional, curriculum-based, strictly-structured method of imparting formal education to children that is followed by most schools around the world today. This method has some quintessential, easily identifiable elements: dividing children into same-age study groups, constantly comparing their progress with their peers, studying subjects in fixed-time slots during the first half of the day; forcing the child to sit still, read, write, and draw during each time slot, and discouraging out-of-context and uninhibited talking and questioning during class - to name but just a few. Forcing the child to stick only to the study of textbooks during "school hours", and rigidly adhering to a timetable and preset schedule are also aspects of the formal schooling approach.

This recreating a 'school' is what I also tried to do at home, and understandably, not only did I get frustrated when it did not go according to my wishes, but I also blamed my own amateur teaching skills for any lack of results. In this time period, I also got stressed out by the rising opposition that my husband and I started to encounter from extended family members. Everyone assumed that we were making a big mistake; that our children would lose out in life and not achieve any academic success. To them, not going to school meant not being educated - period.

In Pakistan, being an overpopulated and underdeveloped country that is struggling on almost all fronts, only street urchins and poor village-dwelling children do not attend school. To married couples in our extended family - who had obtained multiple college degrees - making our children stay at home and not attend school, was a shocking concept for most of them indeed, but for some family members it ignited many emotional and scandalized (not to mention, offensive and disrespectfully accusation-laden) reactions. The road was getting rocky, and the baby steps that we were taking were still in their hesitant, unsure stage. And just then, like a bolt of lightning, yet another cloud came upon us with its hidden silver lining in tow: I got pregnant with my third child!

Third pregnancy: start of unschooling

I must admit that homeschooling can get stressful sometimes, but that happens all the more so if the parents try to strictly replicate the traditional schooling approach at home. All of my early pregnancies were progressively more physically challenging. Which means that the first three to four months of each pregnancy was more taxing for me than the previous one. I became restricted to my bed, getting up just to vomit or to pray. Fighting depression, mood swings, and crankiness became my daily struggle (jihad). I did not leave my home in weeks. I was a weak, irritable, miserable mess. So of course, our homeschooling was put on a hiatus. Confined to my bed, it was then that I started noticing something truly amazing happen right before my eyes, for the first time since becoming a mother: I noticed that my two children, then aged six and four years, still continued to learn!

I was no longer telling them what to do. I could no longer go out to buy them supplies: books, crafts, or other materials. We were homebound, 24/7 for months. Notwithstanding how challenging these difficult months of my pregnancy were for all of us, my children continued to find ways to keep themselves occupied. They would often come to me in the bedroom, showing me what they were making or doing, asking me questions, taking my help, and keeping me involved - at a distance. To top it off, my incapacitated state even facilitated them to prepare their own light snacks and meals: even if it was simple breakfast food throughout the day, such as butter or jam on sliced bread, peeled fruit, or cereal with milk.

I was amazed to see how well they were getting along by living life freely on their own at home, without me hovering like a helicopter homeschooler, instructing them at every step! Sure, they would ask me what to do when they needed to, but by and large, to my utter joy and astonishment, they were getting along just fine in their learning: reading, scribbling, painting, drawing, building with blocks, and engaging in lively, uninhibited imaginative play. They would use apparently useless clutter lying around at home to experiment and improvise, creating self-directed projects based on novel personal ideas. Occasionally, they would even take care of me, by bringing me something that I needed. To put it in a nutshell: this experience proved to be no less than an eye-opening epiphany for me! So we decided, once I recovered and resumed normal life in the middle of my second trimester, that this was the homeschooling model that suited our family perfectly, like a glove: which, I later came to know, is officially referred to as "unschooling".

No stress: living with freedom!
Taking a fish out of water might put it at risk of dying, but not if it wriggles free and dives straight back into an even bigger pond full of a wider plethora of fauna and flora, where it can swim around as it wishes, absolutely free from the risk of attacks by predators, or restrictions of any sort! That is what it feels like for us to unschool our children here in Pakistan, which, due to its lack of stringent laws and law enforcement by the government, ironically provides our family with absolute freedom to do whatever we want with our children, without anyone questioning us or taking us to account for it.

Analogously speaking, it is akin to how a Muslim brought up in a secular country in the West feels when they pray in public or go out to eat at restaurants while visiting a Muslim-majority country for the first time: feeling no need to tone down their Islamic attire or muffle their native language, adopt strange social etiquette, look over their shoulder, brace themselves mentally for stares or awkward glances; and absolutely no need to peer at the packaging of eatables in search of the "halal" label.

Pakistan might have an abundance of shortcomings as a "livable" country according to Western standards, but when it comes to homeschooling children for religiously practicing Muslim families hailing from the middle and upper social classes, it offers an uninhibited, liberating range of options and opportunities. To observe our children running around, playing, creating, building, drawing, eating, laughing, and talking freely, without worrying about bedtimes, homework, exams, peer pressure, or rebuke - that in itself is one of the best things we constantly appreciate about our rewarding choice to unschool them here in the chaotic seaport cosmopolitan city of Karachi.

So, if and when your horizon becomes overcast with clouds, rest assured that there will be a silver lining!

Sadaf Farooqi is an author, blogger and freelance writer based in Karachi, Pakistan, who has been homeschooling her children since 2010. She has two daughters and a son. To date, Sadaf has authored over 300 original articles, most of which can be accessed on her blog, "Sadaf's Space". After her first non-fiction book on Muslim marriage was published by IIPH, she started self-publishing her past articles as non-fiction Islamic books, which are all available on Amazon and Kindle.

Chapter 5
RESOURCES WE LOVE

Review: *Homeschool 101: What To Expect Your First Year*

By Brooke Benoit

If you are considering just keeping your child out of preschool or are looking at the long haul of homeschooling, *Homeschool 101: What to Expect Your First Year* is an indispensable resource for Muslim homeschoolers. If you are still undecided as to if you should homeschool, author Abu Muawiyah Ismail Kamdar's illustration of contemporary schooling's failures and his own reasons for homeschooling are especially convincing – share this book with a doubtful spouse. As he suggests, "Step One: Do your research with your spouse." It's not just Kamdar's solid advice on the practical aspects of homeschooling, his centering of his advice on a deen-based life is what really makes the book helpful.

"Children by their nature are energetic, curious, and playful. The school system tries to kill this but fails miserably. I do not understand why we would want to kill this. It is the nature of the child and it is also a child's strength."

One of the many homeschooling issues Kamdar addresses in a different light is dealing with the parents of potential or new homeschooling parents. While the grandparents' concerns was something I never considered when deciding to homeschool my own children, as Sadaf Farooqi also addresses in this edition of Fitra Journal, extended Muslim families can be deeply involved in a wide range of decision-making for children. Kamdar is on point to advise how to compassionately and effectively deal with them. He also does a great job of explaining children's dispositions and psychology, and that parents need to learn how to work well with children instead of following many of the poor authoritative or permissive styles of parenting modelled to many of us. Kamdar is even frank that not all parents are fit to homeschool. He includes plenty of warnings about difficult areas of homeschooling, which I haven't seen elsewhere, perhaps in attempt to not scare homeschoolers off, Allahualim.

"A homeschooling house will have noise, it will get messy, it will have moments of chaos, but it will also be fun full of memories, and a joyful bonding experience for parent and child alike."

One issue that is especially astute of Kamdar to address is part of what I call the Homeschool Prodigy Myth, "When one begins homeschooling, it is very easy to get caught up in the zeal and excitement of things and want to learn and teach every day all day long. This method however is not productive and will lead to burnout." Yes! On a couple of occasions I have hired overzealous tutors who either thought they were playing school instead of focusing on the one subject they were hired for or maybe they were just so excited to have their own clumps of clay to mold, but nope - being homeschooled shouldn't be mistaken for having endless hours to dump every and all information possible into your child's little repository. Really, I think this is a common pitfall, I have seen my husband and even my children do this with peer-tutoring. It can be easy to get caught up in the moment and the possibilities, and not even be able to see your child's disinterest and both you getting very frustrated. For most work sessions, I find it helpful to have a goal of 40 minutes with flexibility to go over that time if things are really gelling, but there will be those days when you find yourself just burnt-out and going nowhere, later realizing you were at it for far too long.

With homeschooling mostly being the realm of moms' doing, it is great to hear from such a knowledgeable and involved homeschooling father. This is one area I would especially like to hear Kamdar speak more to, insha Allah - the father's role in homeschooling. Kamdar also writes extensively on issues around self-help, time management and positivity, his works are available through http://islamicselfhelp.com/ebook-store/

Review: Miraj Audio

By Chantal Blake

I can only remember a single audio story from my childhood. It was a read-along cassette that accompanied my favorite story *If You Give a Mouse a Cookie* by Laura Joffe Numeroff and Felicia Bond. The simple, playful illustrations entertained me while listening to the text being read by a pleasant, feminine voice. I also recall the sound of chimes indicating when to turn the pages. I never imagined that an audio story could be engaging and compelling enough to stand alone without a book, but this is exactly what I've found with Miraj audiobooks.

It was an unusually cold and wet winter in Casablanca when we discovered Miraj Audio. Most days, a bowl of porridge and cuddling by the space heater were all that could warm us while watching the dreary skies from our window-paned French doors. But on the day that a friend recommended a free audio story download, our mornings became much brighter.

Our first story, *The Sad Camel*, took us to Arabia to meet Ibil, a neglected camel who was overworked and distraught. His careless owner abused him until the Prophet (SAW) met Ibil and demanded to know the perpetrator of such negligence and abuse. The story, inspired by an authentic hadith, reminded us of how our beloved Prophet's concern and care not only encompassed human lives but extended to include animals too. My daughter was touched by this tender side of her Messenger (SAW) and asked to hear the stories again and again. When she started anticipating the lines of the story, we knew it was time to try another.

Leyla the Sparrow, The Prophet and the Ants, and *Nuh and the Flood* are all creatively narrated from the perspective of animals who interacted with messengers of Allah. The stories are crafted with sound effects and tunes that make the listening experience as captivating as a movie but limitless in imagination. One story titled *A Gift to the Sands* is told by a pearl who never meets a prophet but still teaches us a valuable lesson about pride and arrogance. Some of the stories for older children detail dramatic Quranic events like *Yusuf and His Amazing Dreams* or brave tales from Islamic history like *Salah ad-Din and the Wicked Prince*. An upcoming story takes the liberty of reinventing Cinderella to become her Muslim equivalent, *Noor*.

Behind the success of Miraj Audio as the first independent digital publisher of Islamic books for children in English, you'll find two sincere parents and their story-loving son. His fascination with audiobooks was initially sated by fantasy tales. Wanting to impart more ethical values, his parents sought Islamic audio recordings but could only found high-quality narratives of Biblical stories. With their combined skills as an audio designer and radio producer, they rose to the challenge of developing the caliber of Islamic stories they had been looking for. Assisted by an elaborate professional team of writers, editors, narrators, audio engineers, sound designers, illustrators, scholars, and educators, they have succeeded in their goal to use "the power of storytelling to help children experience the beauty of Islam and engage with its values and tradition".

Whether as a backdrop for breakfast in the morning, a companion on a long road trip, or a healthy substitute for TV, Miraj Audio stories can be an ally in your homeschooling and life learning. They succeed in appealing to a child's curiosity and interest while stirring some new idea in their mind or noble motive in their heart. Available affordably by download or cd, with or without music, it won't be hard to discover a story that will soon become your child's favorite and yours too.

Miraj audiobooks are available at www.mirajaudio.com.

Fitra Contributors' Ultimate Resources

Zakiya Mahomed-Kalla's Favorite Resources for Arabic and Islamic Studies:
Islamic School Book series by Goodword Books

Yassarnal Qur'aan series

The Youtube channel "Learning Roots" features many stories of the prophets (peace be upon them)

One4kids.net features "Zaky-TV", which offers videos on the stories of the Prophets; learning dua, Arabic, and even how to perform salaah; and other Islamic concepts. It is aimed at young children. Apps for Android and Apple devices can also be downloaded, which feature games and quizzes on Islamic knowledge. These games can also be played on the main website of one4kids.net

Artists Zain Bhikha, Yusuf Islam, and Dawud Wharnsby are just a few who have made songs for Muslim children. An example of a great song to help kids remember the Arabic alphabet is "A is for Allah" by Zain Bhikha.

Klaudia Khan's Favorites for Young Children:
My children love the OKIDO books, especially the titles *My Head to Toe Body Book* and. They look great as they are colourful, bright, and amusingly illustrated, which attracts children's attention straight away. Besides, they are full of interesting activities fitted just right for children aged three to six. And they are pretty useful in teaching about bones, muscles and blood circulation (*My Head to Toe Body Book*), as everything is explained in lovely pictures and a few simple sentences.

For Islamic studies we love the Goodword publications. Currently we are reading *365 Days with Prophet Muhammad (SAW)*. It's a very child-friendly seerah. It is illustrated, but not excessively, so it is perfect for reading at bedtime. We also enjoy the *Quran Explorer*, which has fun puzzles and activities, too.

Another favourite is *The Story of the Elephant* book from Shade 7. My younger daughter wants to read it every other day for a year now! It also has some activities and it is the perfect way to teach children the stories from the Qur'an. Can't wait for more of these to come, in'sha'Allah.

Our favourite art 'teacher' is Mr Herve Tullet. His colouring book is full of inspirational ideas and fun activities, it is actually much more than a colouring book. There is also *The Art Workshops for Children* book by the same author, which I am planning to purchase soon, insha Allah.

We don't use much technology in our homeschooling, so here are few others of our favourite titles: *Maps* by Mizielinska - great for learning basic geography and exploring the culture of other countries, Usborne phonics readers - the best phonic readers we came across, they actually tell a story, have fun lift-the-flaps and good illustrations, *Nature Anatomy* is an adult picture book that we all enjoy. *Tinkerlab* is great for simple and fun science and art activities.

Asma Ali's Must Haves for Homeschoolers:
Reading Lesson: Teach Your Child to Read in 20 Easy Lessons - Just ten minutes a day with this book set my son well on his way to reading with ease. With clear instructions for the parent as you go through each lesson, pictures to break up the text and engaging activities, this book is simple, effective and enjoyable.

Artfulparent.com - An excellent resource on all things arts and crafts for toddlers and upwards! You don't need to be the most creative whizz around to enjoy this (check out the 'parents corner' to help you get started).

Pinterest - From DIY puffy paint to projects with a cardboard box, there's something for everyone. Now this is a bandwagon definitely worth jumping on. The amount of resources is immense! With a quick search, you'll find free printables and ideas for whatever stage of homeschooling you are at.*

Brooke Benoit's Picks:
Books for early childhood education - *You Are Your Child's First Teacher: Encouraging Your Child's Natural Development from Birth to Age Six* by Rahima Baldwin Dancy

The Heart of Learning and *Oak Meadow Guide to Teaching Early Grades* by Oak Meadow.

Our favourite informative internet media - BrainPOP.com and the YouTube channels In a Nutshell, MinuteEarth and Vsauce.

Sadaf Farooqi's Unschooling essentials:
Goodword Books, Starfall.com, Hiba Magazine & HibaKidz, V-Shine Magazine, Lego & Duplo, and Bricks and Meccano

*Be sure to look for the Fitra Journal pin board!

Quranhearts.wordpress.com

is a blog for hearts who hold the Qur'an, or aspire to. We welcome creative contributions as we aim to be a fully-fledged website dedicated to remembering the Qur'an, for the pleasure of Allah.

Qur'an Hearts: Hearts on a quest for enlightenment

REBOOT YOUR LIFE

Confessions of a Muslim Mom

... your mind
... your habits
... your life

confessionsofamuslimmommaholic.com

www.azramomin.com
ART - ILLUSTRATIONS - TEXTILE WORK

For commissions and collaborations contact Azra at azra@azramomin.com

Are you struggling with confidence issues?

Are you looking for an Islamic method to increase confidence?

Best Of Creation is a 200 page e-book guide to building your confidence the Islamic way.

Download it today for just $6.99!

Instant download Eid Cards by Samar Asamoah to send to your family and friends.

Eid Mubarak

All proceeds go to Syria.
www.yezarck.com/shop

Now you can purchase Sadaf Farooqi's non-fiction Islamic books on Amazon.com & Kindle!

PLEASE VISIT: WWW.AMAZON.COM/AUTHOR/SADAFFAROOQI

Learn *Organically*

Exploring educational options for your families? Try Oak Meadow! We provide flexible, creative homeschooling curriculum for grades K to 12.

- K-8 is child-centered, nature-based, hands-on
- High School offers life experience credit, independent study, dual enrollment, college counseling
- Start anytime during the year

NEW at Oak Meadow

- **Digital curriculum now available for K-8:** Replication of our high quality print curriculum, delivered in a digital format.
- **Foundations in Independent Learning:** A practical and inspiring online teacher training program designed for parents and teachers who support independent learners.

Save May 8-30
15% off in our Bookstore

INDEPENDENT LEARNING SINCE 1975

visit oakmeadow.com

www.ingramcontent.com/pod-product-compliance
Lightning Source LLC
Chambersburg PA
CBHW070548300426
44113CB00011B/1823